KOREAN COOKING

KOREAN COOKING

EXPLORE ONE OF THE ORIENT'S GREATEST CULINARY SECRETS

HILAIRE WALDEN

CHARTWELL BOOKS, INC.

A QUINTET BOOK

Published by Chartwell Books
A Division of Book Sales, Inc.
PO Box 7100
Edison, New Jersey 08818-7100

This edition produced for sale in the U.S.A., its
territories and dependencies only.

ISBN 0-7858-0268-1

This book was designed and produced by
Quintet Publishing Limited
6 Blundell Street
London N7 9BH

Creative Director: Richard Dewing
Designer: Ian Hunt
Project Editor: Anna Briffa
Editor: Susan Martineau
Photographer: Nick Bailey
Home Economist: Kit Chan

Typeset in Great Britain by
Central Southern Typesetters, Eastbourne
Manufactured in China by
Regent Publishing Services Ltd
Printed in China by Leefung-Asco Printers Ltd

There are at least two widely used forms for
transliterating written Korean (even in Korea
inconsistencies can occur). The main accepted
form is the McCane-Reichauer and it is this that has
been followed, as far as possible, in this book.

ACKNOWLEDGMENTS
Pictures courtesy of Korea National Tourism
Corporation (pages 6, 8, 15, 36, 39, 42, 49, 61, 65,
77, 91, 92, 101, 114, 119)
The Publisher would like to thank Také Ltd,
London, for providing props for photography

CONTENTS

INTRODUCTION

Korea is rarely thought of as a beautiful country, yet it has superb scenery – plunging waterfalls, verdant paddy fields, cedar forests, Mongolian desert, and wide, sea-lapped beaches. Its walled villages have reddish-brown, tiled roofs of locally made stone. Many of the old traditions still survive and in country areas, the men still wear stovepipe hats and baggy trousers tied at the ankles. In the cities the old rubs shoulders with the new. Seoul, the capital of South Korea, is a high-rise city crisscrossed with multiple highways which overshadow walled temples and old royal palaces. In the six-story East Gate Market over 15,000 shoppers a day visit walkways where cooked pigs' heads, squid and fresh chickens are sold beside quilted cushions and bolts of colored silk.

BELOW *An open market. A rich variety of grains and pulses is available.*

Over the centuries Korea has been the focus of much aggressive attention from her neighbors, and each wave of intruders has left a mark on Korean cuisine.

As early as 100 B.C. Chinese colonies were burgeoning around the peninsula to the extent that Silla, in the south of ancient Korea, called itself with some pride, "Little China." Ancient Korea, in fact, comprised three kingdoms: Koguryo in the North; Paekche and Silla in the South. They were all culturally advanced, and had a centralized government, royal courts, nobility and a class system. A unified country was established after the kingdom of Silla, assisted by the Chinese, conquered first Paekche and then Koguryo. In this new country there were five provincial capitals administered by a sophisticated civil service. There were also splendid grand palaces, elaborate temples and tombs, and imposing monuments.

Then, in the thirteenth century, Genghis Khan's Mongol hordes swept over the country.

In 1876 Korea concluded a trade treaty with Japan, much to the alarm of China. Europeans had started to arrive after the mid-seventeenth century, and after the signing of the Japanese treaty, others were agreed with European countries and the United States.

In 1910, Japan annexed Korea and retained rule over her until after the end of World War II. From China and Japan, Korea adopted the principle of the five flavors – sweet, sour, hot, salty and bitter – and the practice of spending more time cutting, slicing and dicing ingredients, especially vegetables, than cooking them. The Korean version of the wok, the *sot*, is also a legacy of the Chinese, and the presence of the Mongols is still apparent in the predeliction for table-top cooking.

Topography and climate determine to a large extent the foods naturally available and the type of dishes that are cooked. Being surrounded on three sides by water, fish is important in Korean cuisine. There is an almost endless supply of fish and shellfish – red snapper, skate, sole, pollack, tuna, herring, cod, croaker, horse mackerel, corvina, oysters, shrimp, clams, abalone, mussels, sea snails and sea cucumber, to name just some. The cold, deep Sea of Japan off the east coast provides the deepwater varieties such as squid and cuttlefish, while the shallower Yellow Sea that stretches away toward China supplies those that thrive in warmer waters.

The shores are also a source of sea vegetables which the Koreans have enjoyed eating for centuries, for example, kelp, laver and seaweed.

The mountains that occupy much of the country provide a selection of wild vegetables, mushrooms, herbs and roots. The lowlands and plains of the south support large areas of agriculture. Modern food production techniques have enabled South Korea to increase the cultivation and yields of vegetables, grains and fruits, and today enough rice and corn are grown to satisfy the country's needs. Vegetables like sweet and white potatoes, carrots, soybeans, white radishes, Chinese cabbage, scallions and red bell peppers, flavorful fruits such as apples, plums, peaches, grapes and luscious strawberries, nuts and grains, are cultivated. Semi-tropical Cheju Island supplies tangerines and oranges.

As you travel farther south, the food becomes hotter, spicier and more salty. Unusually for an eastern Asian country, beef is the most popular meat (pork and chicken usually reign supreme). This liking for beef is said to be a legacy of Mongolian ancestors. Mongol tribes first migrated south from what is now Manchuria in prehistoric times, but it was the warring, pillaging, thirteenth-century Mongol armies who decided the best place to raise cattle was on the rich pastures of Cheju Island. The practice continues today. Now, the pastures are divided into American-style ranges, some as large as 200,000 acres, and the cattle are just as likely to be Western Charolais, Aberdeen Angus and Hereford as local breeds.

Korea has hot summers with plentiful rain (ideal for much agriculture, particularly rice), but bitterly cold winters. These have given rise to the Korean tradition of preserving fish and vegetables to provide food during the lean months. All manner of fish and shellfish, such as anchovies, shrimp, oysters, pollack, cuttlefish and octopus, are pickled, salted and dried, while vegetables are pickled and turned into *kimchi*. Every fall, in the country vast amounts of vegetables are harvested to make

ABOVE *Popular at every mealtime, Kimchis are prepared in vast quantities.*

large batches of a wide range of different *kimchi*s. These are then packed into enormous earthenware jars that are buried in the ground outside and left until required. Although the necessity for so much preservation does not exist nowadays, Koreans still make their traditional preserves because they enjoy eating them so much. Also, salted shrimp and oysters are a common addition to *kimchi* as they increase the mineral content and enrich the flavor; they dissolve during the fermentation and do not give a fishy taste.

Every house will also have its *jang* terrace. In the country this will be a stone area outside, but in towns and cities a balcony or flat roof will have to suffice. On the *jang* terrace stand large earthenware jars of basic ingredients used in every Korean kitchen – *kanjang* (soy sauce), *twoenjang* (fermented soybean paste) and *kochujang* (chili bean paste). Cooks used to ferment their own beans to make these condiments, but now the sauces are usually bought ready-made.

Social factors also influence who eats what, and how they eat it. As Korea has a long-established hierarchical system, there is a deep-seated division between the elaborate, rich and more sophisticated foods of the courts and upper classes such as *Shinsollo* and *Kujolpan* (see page 26) and the robust, hearty fare of the people.

Food is associated with the many Korean festivals. Rice cakes and taro soup are served for New Year's, and chrysanthemum cakes and wine for the ninth day of the ninth month. Fruit, wine and cakes are taken on a special date to ancestors' graves, and on its first birthday a child sits amidst biscuits, rice cakes and fruit. The sixty-first birthday is also cause for celebration. Sixty is traditionally regarded as the average life-span, so to have survived one year more is an accomplishment to warrant a grand celebratory feast.

EATING KOREAN-STYLE

As in other Far Eastern countries, such as China, Thailand and Japan, Koreans sit around a low table to eat. Every person has their own rice bowl, traditionally made of brass and usually lidded. Long, pencil-thin metal chopsticks are used for eating, with a metal spoon for soups.

All the dishes for a meal are served at once, and often, particularly for dinner, the main meal of the day, there will be quite a few. A simple family dinner, for example, might include some 20 *panchan* (side dishes) containing a tempting array of *namuls* (seasoned raw or lightly cooked vegetables); *nibles* such as dried vegetables and shrimp, salted fish, roast seaweed; dipping sauces and *kimchi* (at least one type of these is essential and preferably there should be three or four). Soup is also an essential element of every meal, and there are also likely to be some *jon* (flour- and egg-coated fried vegetables). Even more substantial fish, meat and poultry dishes are served in what would be considered small amounts in the West. With such variety on offer large portions of any one thing are unnecessary.

Lunch is a lighter meal of noodles or rice mixed with vegetables, or another grain or beans for protein. Breakfast is traditionally almost as large as dinner but, nowadays, it tends to be lighter. Even so, there will be at least rice, soup and *kimchi*. In the cities, smaller Western-style breakfasts are becoming more popular.

Slurping while eating is considered an indication that the food is being enjoyed, and a good belch afterwards is a sign of having eaten well. However, blowing the nose at table is a grave social misdemeanor (an offender is demoted to the status of a *sangnom* – an unperson).

EQUIPMENT

As it is the cuisine of country people, preparing Korean food requires only simple, limited equipment and little in the way of complicated skills. It does, however, take a long time to prepare a traditional Korean meal because it contains so many different dishes.

The traditional Korean kitchen is situated at or below ground. Cooking is done on a two- or four-burner stove plate that is fueled by anthracite. Pipes run from the stove under the floor of the living areas of houses to provide a system of central heating.

RICE COOKER Because of the amount of rice that is eaten, city dwellers now use electric rice cookers as they cook rice perfectly every time and will keep the rice hot,

KNIVES Preparing Korean food takes much time-consuming chopping and slicing, so good-quality sharp knives are most important. A food processor, mandoline slicer or grater can be used and, for wafer-thin slices, a potato peeler. A sharp knife is also necessary for slicing and scoring meat and poultry.

HANDS Koreans often use their hands for mixing, for example, ingredients for a marinade, and for beating eggs as less air is incorporated.

TABLE-TOP COOKER Koreans are very fond of cooking food at table. For this, small table-top burners fueled by small butane gas canisters are often used. Metal grids are used for cooking the food directly over the flame.

SHINSOLLO A special bronze or brass pot is used for preparing the dish of the same name. The pot has a central funnel in which hot charcoal is placed to keep the food hot.

THE FLAVORS OF KOREAN COOKING

Garlic, chilies, ginger, scallions, sesame oil and sesame seeds – these provide the staple and stable character of Korean food and at least one will appear in nearly every dish. In addition there are other ingredients essential to Korean cooking, some of which follow.

BEAN CURD

White, milky, thick custard-like bean curd, also known as tofu, is made from soybeans, and is high in protein and low in fat. Bean curd is widely used in Korean cooking; it is served on its own after being sautéd, deep-fried or braised, added to soups, casseroles and braised dishes.

Fresh bean curd can be made at home (see page 114) or bought from healthfood and ethnic stores. It usually comes in three textures – soft, medium and firm. It is best eaten on the day it is bought, or made, but may be stored in a container, covered by cold water and refrigerated for 2–3 days; change the water every day.

CHILIES

CHILIES

Ripe, red chilies are used in Korea. There are many different varieties of chili and each variety has its own flavor and hotness; size is not an infallible guide to hotness, but generally the larger the chili, the less intense the heat. Chopping a chili increases the amount of "fire" in a dish, as does including the seeds. Chilies add flavor as well as hotness, so, for a milder dish, instead of reducing the number of chilies used, leave the chilies whole, if possible, and discard the seeds. Chilies are also painstakingly cut into fine shreds for using as a garnish in Korean cooking.

Chilies should be handled carefully as they contain a substance that can irritate the skin. If you have a cut, bruise or lesion on your hands, or your skin is sensitive, wear thin rubber gloves when preparing chilies.

CHILI POWDER

Korean chili powder is among the best in the world. It is relatively mild, a glowing carmine color and coarsely pounded. It tastes somewhat like a cross between paprika and cayenne pepper (which can be used as a substitute if

TOFU

necessary). It is added to dishes with generosity, not only flavoring them and adding "heat," but giving them a characteristic glorious vibrant color.

GARLIC

Garlic goes into a great many savory dishes. Koreans like their garlic to have impact – in stir-fry dishes it is added at the end, not the beginning of the cooking (the pungency diminishes during cooking), and cloves may be pounded, then finely chopped, to release the maximum flavor. Koreans also eat whole, peeled cloves – dishes of them are put on restaurant tables to be nibbled neat or cooked on a table-top broiler. Most Korean markets and supermarkets sell ready-peeled garlic.

GARLIC

GINGER

GINGER

Ginger is a very popular addition to many Korean dishes. Choose plump fresh ginger so there is a high proportion of flesh to skin, and make sure it feels firm and has a shiny skin.

KIMCHI

Kimchi is the spicy national pickle. It is ubiquitous. Not only is it considered a vital part of every meal, including breakfast, but is added to soups, stews, stir-fries and pancakes. You do not have to make your own (see pages 40–64) as bottles of *kimchi* can be bought from Korean grocery stores and supermarkets.

There are many different types of *kimchi* – in the Seoul museum devoted entirely to *kimchi*, there are 160 different versions, such as Chinese leaf, white radish, cucumber, stuffed cucumber, garlic, Chinese turnip and onion.

KOCHUJANG

Kochujang is Korea's red, spicy version of a chili bean paste. It is an essential seasoning and serves as a cross between a relish and a spice. *Kochujang* is added to meats that are to be stir-fried, stews and dips, and served in small bowls as a sweet, spicy, hot relish.

In every household in Korea there is a tall earthenware jar of thick, red *kochujang* – its preparation is lengthy and elaborate, using glutinous rice powder or barley mixed with malt, then cooking it slowly to a smooth, thick paste. This is mixed with fermented chili powder, soybean powder and salt.

Kochujang can also be bought ready-made in jars in Korea. In the West it is only available from Korean supermarkets. An improvised version can be made at home (see page 69), or you can use Chinese chili bean paste available at most supermarkets.

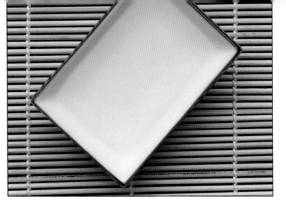

RICE VINEGAR

CELLOPHANE NOODLES

NOODLES

Cellophane noodles These are also known as bean thread or transparent noodles. They are made from ground mung beans and are clear-white, fine, dried strands that are so tough they are almost impossible to cut. They are sold in bundles and need to be soaked for 10–15 minutes before cooking. After cooking cellophane noodles become soft, slippery and gelatinous.

    Buckwheat noodles Korean buckwheat noodles, *son myon*, are very thin dried noodles. Japanese *shoba* noodles are also made from buckwheat but are fatter; Japanese *somen* noodles or Italian vermicelli or capellini are nearer in size to Korean buckwheat noodles, but they are made from wheat flour.

RICE VINEGAR

For the recipes in this book use Japanese rice vinegar, which is lighter and milder than Chinese brands. White wine vinegar can be substituted, or dilute 3 parts white distilled vinegar with 1 part water; if the recipe does not include sugar, add a small pinch.

RICE WINE

Rice wine is a light, slightly sweet wine. Use dry sherry if it is not available.

SESAME OIL

SESAME OIL

In Korea, sesame oil is used as a flavoring as well as for cooking. The sesame oil used in Korea is made from toasted sesame seeds, so has an amber color and nutty sesame flavor. As it therefore provides a characteristic flavor as well as color, using pale sesame oil instead will not give authentic-tasting dishes. Keep sesame oil in a cool, dark place.

BLACK AND WHITE SESAME SEEDS

SESAME SEEDS

Sesame seeds are used in such quantities that they are often bought by the tubful in the fall soon after harvesting, when the price is at its lowest. Small quantities of sesame seeds are roasted at a time in a heavy, dry pan, then lightly crushed with salt (see page 22). These are added to sauces, marinades, dips and salads, as well as braised dishes. Black sesame seeds have a more pronounced, and slightly more bitter taste than white sesame seeds. They are also used in Chinese and Japanese cookery.

SEA VEGETABLES

Dried kelp is a green, calcium-rich sea vegetable resembling large, long leaves. Called *tasima* in Korean, it is also known by its Japanese name, *konbu* or *kombu*. It is available either folded or cut into small pieces. A fine white salty deposit forms on the surface; this should not be washed off as the flavor of kelp is near the surface. Instead, wipe with a damp cloth just before using.

KELP AND WAKAME

Dried laver is also well known by its Japanese name, *nori*; the Korean name is *kim*. It is thin, crisp and vitamin- and mineral-packed. There are many varieties and qualities, from dark green to purplish black and from medium-priced to expensive; price is usually a good guide to quality. Like dried kelp, dried laver is available from healthfood stores as well as ethnic stores, and is generally sold in sheets about 7 by 8 inches. Store dried laver in an airtight container.

Before dried laver is eaten, it is passed over a flame several times until it becomes crisp (see page 29). It may then be eaten as it is or crumbled over noodle or rice dishes.

Dried seaweed A green type of seaweed, often known by its Japanese name of *wakame*, is used in Korea in soups and stews, and dressed with a vinegar dressing in salads. When dried, *wakame* darkens. It is sold in small packages in healthfood and ethnic stores. Before using, it should be soaked for about 30 minutes, after which time some of its former color returns and it becomes fairly slippery.

RICE

Korean rice is a medium- to short-grain variety that becomes sticky when cooked (see page 102). It is available from Korean grocery stores and supermarkets, but if you are not able to find it, substitute Japanese rice.

RICE

LIGHT AND DARK SOYBEAN PASTE

SOY SAUCE

Soy sauce is an essential flavoring and seasoning. Light, medium and dark soy sauces are available; light versions tend to be the thinnest and most salty. Japanese soy sauce (medium) has been used for all of the recipes in this book.

SCALLIONS

A variety of shapes and sizes of scallion is found in Korea, but the most common are larger than typical Western scallions. Use the plumpest you can find for the recipes in this book (Middle Eastern stores often sell fatter, plumper scallions).

SOYBEAN PASTE

Soybean paste is made from fermented soybean cakes, pepper and salt. This thick brown paste has a pungent, characteristic flavor. Japanese miso can be used as a substitute.

CHINESE MUSHROOMS AND WOOD EAR FUNGUS

CHINESE MUSHROOMS

These are black or brown dried mushrooms. Long ago the Chinese discovered that drying them intensifies their flavor. They should be soaked in water for about 20 minutes, then squeezed to get rid of the salt. Wood Ear Fungus is another form of dried mushroom, valued for its subtle, delicate flavor and slightly crunchy "bite." When soaked, it expands to five times its dried size.

SOY SAUCE

SOUPS AND FIRST COURSES

Soups are an important component of every proper Korean meal, even breakfast, but soup is not eaten at the beginning of the meal, as in the West; instead it is served with the other dishes. Although traditional Korean meals do not feature a first course (all the dishes are served at once), there are recipes that are suitable for serving at the beginning of Western-style meals. Koreans are very fond of nibbling, especially when they are drinking; the abundant drinking houses (*suljip*) have an array of snacks on offer to their customers in the hope of increasing the drinking rate, in a similar way to Spanish *tapas* bars. These snacks can also be served at home to accompany drinks, instead of chips and peanuts, or for a light first course.

SPINACH SOUP

Shikumchiguk

This is a favorite soup throughout South Korea.

SERVES 3-4

5 ounces chicken breast, thinly sliced and cut into
   1-inch cubes
3 scallions, finely chopped
2 garlic cloves, chopped
2 tablespoons soy sauce
1½ teaspoons sesame seeds
freshly ground black pepper
1½ tablespoons vegetable oil
5½ cups Korean Chicken Stock (see below)
12 ounces fresh spinach, trimmed and shredded
sesame oil for sprinkling

❖ Mix the chicken with the scallions, garlic, soy sauce, sesame seeds and plenty of pepper. Leave for 30 minutes.

❖ Heat the vegetable oil in a large saucepan. Add the chicken mixture and fry until browned. Add the chicken stock and heat until just simmering. Simmer very slowly for about 25 minutes until the chicken is tender.

❖ Add the spinach and cook for 2–5 minutes more until the spinach is tender. Adjust the seasonings; if the liquid has reduced too much, add hot water as necessary.

❖ Serve sprinkled with sesame oil.

KOREAN CHICKEN STOCK

Dack Kukmul

The garlic cloves can be left whole, cut into halves or chopped, according to how pronounced you want the flavor to be.

MAKES ABOUT 5 CUPS

1 chicken carcass, preferably with skin,
   or about 1½–2 pounds raw or cooked chicken
   trimmings, bones and skin
3 thin slices of fresh ginger
2 garlic cloves (optional)
2 scallions, white and some green parts split
   lengthways

❖ Put the chicken into a large saucepan. Add 7½ cups water and bring slowly to a boil. Skim the scum from the surface. Add the garlic, ginger and split scallions. Cover and simmer for about 3 hours.

❖ Drain through a strainer lined with cheesecloth. Leave until cold, then put in the refrigerator until set. Remove the fat from the surface. Cover and keep in the refrigerator for up to 4 days; boil every other day.

SEAWEED SOUP

Miyoguk

Wrap the meat and put it in the freezer for about 35 minutes to make cutting it into strips easier. *Wakame* is the Japanese name for a green type of seaweed available dried in packages from healthfood and ethnic stores.

SERVES 6

4 ounces dried *wakame*, soaked for at least 30 minutes

6¼ cups fish or beef stock

1 bunch scallions, white and some green parts chopped

1 tablespoon sesame oil

1 garlic clove, crushed and finely chopped

6 ounces lean tender beef, cut into fine strips

soy sauce

toasted sesame seeds for garnish

❖ Drain the wakame and cut it into strips.

❖ Pour the stock into a saucepan. Add the scallions and bring to a boil. Lower the heat so the stock simmers slowly. Heat the oil in a skillet. Add the garlic and beef and stir-fry for about 2 minutes. Add to the stock together with the wakame. Add soy sauce to taste and heat through. Serve garnished with toasted sesame seeds.

CHICKEN SOUP WITH CLAMS AND SPINACH

Takguk

Shellfish and poultry have a natural affinity. Here, chicken and clams are combined with great success, and the union is enhanced by spinach.

SERVES 4

16 clams

1 tablespoon vegetable oil

2 garlic cloves, crushed and finely chopped

1½–2 teaspoons finely chopped fresh ginger

3 scallions, white and some green parts chopped

1 chicken breast, cut into very fine strips

3¾ cups Korean Chicken Stock (see page 16)

12 ounces fresh spinach, chopped

1½ teaspoons sesame oil

salt and freshly ground black pepper

❖ Scrub the clams and rinse them under running cold water.

❖ Heat the vegetable oil in a saucepan. Add the garlic, ginger, scallions and chicken, and stir-fry for 30 seconds. Add the chicken stock and bring to a boil. Simmer for 5 minutes.

❖ Add the clams. Return to a boil and simmer for 3–5 minutes until the clam shells open; discard any that remain closed. Stir in the spinach. Simmer for 1–2 minutes, then remove the pan from the heat. Add the sesame oil and season to taste.

White Radish Soup ▶

WHITE RADISH SOUP

Kakguk

This warming, soothing soup is usually served for breakfast.

SERVES 4-6

16 dried Chinese mushrooms, soaked in
   hot water for 30 minutes

6¼ cups Korean Chicken Stock (see page 16)

1 pound diced white radish

10 ounces mung bean sprouts

1 teaspoon soy sauce

½ teaspoon sugar

freshly ground black pepper

❖ Remove the mushrooms from the soaking water. Drain and reserve the water.

❖ Remove and discard the stalks from the mushrooms. Thinly slice the caps and put into a large saucepan with the stock. Bring to a boil and add the white radish. Cover the saucepan and simmer slowly for about 10 minutes until the white radish is tender.

❖ Add the bean sprouts, return to a boil. Cover again and simmer for 3–4 minutes more. Add the soy sauce, sugar and pepper.

DUMPLING SOUP

Manduguk

Korean dumpling soup is nothing like a European soup with dumplings, but contains small dumplings filled with water chestnuts, pork and chicken, like Chinese *dim sum*.

SERVES 6

1 carrot, chopped

1 onion, chopped

1 garlic clove, chopped

6 water chestnuts, chopped

4 ounces lean pork

4 ounces chicken

1 cup cooked, shelled shrimp

2 tablespoons soy sauce

1 tablespoon sesame oil

**pinch of Korean chili powder, or cayenne
    pepper mixed with paprika**

30 wonton wrappers

7½ cups Korean Chicken Stock (see page 16)

scallions, chopped, to garnish

❖ Put the vegetables and three-quarters of the pork, chicken and shrimp in a food processor. Dice the remaining pork, chicken and shrimp. Add the soy sauce, sesame oil and a pinch of Korean chili powder, or cayenne pepper mixed with paprika, to the food processor, and mix to a smooth paste.

❖ Spoon a little of the vegetable mixture into each wonton wrapper. Wet the edges and draw together to make a neat bundle. Pinch the edges together to seal.

❖ Bring the stock to a boil in a saucepan. Add the dumplings and diced pork, chicken and shrimp. Simmer for 8–10 minutes. Garnish with scallions before serving.

COLD BUCKWHEAT NOODLE SOUP

Naengmyon

This soup is almost a meal in itself. Because of the number of elements which have to be prepared separately, it may appear to be a complicated recipe, but, in fact, each vegetable is simple to prepare and all of them can be done ahead.

SERVES 4

8 ounces buckwheat noodles

5 cups Korean Chicken Stock (see page 16)

I teaspoon sesame oil

½ long cucumber, thinly sliced

salt

1½ teaspoons rice vinegar

pinch of sugar

pinch of Korean chili powder, or cayenne pepper
    mixed with paprika

2 hard-cooked eggs, shelled and thinly sliced

8 pieces of white radish, cut into thin strips

½ Korean (Asian) pear, peeled, cored and
    thinly sliced

I cup liquid from white radish

selection of Dipping Sauces (see sesame page 58,
    vinegar page 32 and ginger page 35) to serve

❖ Cook the noodles according to the instructions on the package. Drain and rinse under running cold water. Drain well, then put into a bowl and toss with ½ cup of the stock, and the sesame oil.

❖ Put the cucumber slices in a colander and toss with salt. Leave for 1 hour. Rinse the cucumber well, drain and dry thoroughly on paper towels. Mix with the rice vinegar, sugar and chili powder, or cayenne pepper mixed with paprika.

❖ Divide the noodles between four dishes. Pour one quarter of the remaining stock into each dish. Arrange a few neatly overlapping slices of egg around the top of each pile of noodles. Surround with slightly overlapping vegetable and pear slices.

BEEF SOUP

Mou-kuk

Korean turnips are large and round. Substitute two small round turnips
if the Korean variety are not available.

SERVES 6

1½ pounds braising beef

1 Korean turnip or 2 small round turnips, peeled

2½ tablespoons sesame oil

2 garlic cloves, crushed and finely chopped

4 scallions, white and some green parts chopped

1 teaspoon sugar

1 tablespoon Crushed Toasted Sesame Seeds
  (see below)

1½ tablespoons Korean chili powder, or cayenne
  pepper mixed with paprika

1½ tablespoons soy sauce

salt (optional)

❖ Put the beef and turnip in a saucepan with
6¼ cups water. Bring to a boil. Skim the scum
from the surface, then cover the pan and
simmer gently for 1½–2 hours until the meat is
very tender. Remove from the heat and leave
the beef and turnip to cool in the liquid.

❖ Skim the fat from the surface of the liquid
and remove the beef and turnip. Thinly slice the
turnip and finely chop the beef.

❖ Heat the sesame oil in a saucepan. Add the
garlic and scallions, and fry for 2 minutes. Stir
in the beef, turnip, sugar, sesame seeds, chili
powder, or cayenne mixed with paprika, and
soy sauce, and cook for a couple of minutes.
Add to the stock and heat through, 5 minutes.

CRUSHED TOASTED SESAME SEEDS

Prepare the quantity of these that is appropriate to the amount of Korean
cooking you are going to do (it is easy to increase or halve the recipe),
and store them in a screw-top jar in a cool, dark place.

⅓ cup sesame seeds

2 teaspoons salt

❖ Heat a small, heavy skillet over a medium-
low heat. Add the sesame seeds and stir until
they darken a shade and give off a toasted, nutty
aroma.

❖ Crush the seeds with the salt in a pestle and
mortar. Keep in a screw-top jar.

MUNG BEAN PANCAKES

Pindaetuk

Pindaetuk are a popular street snack, but they are also made in restaurants and homes for celebratory occasions such as birthdays, weddings and New Year's. The street versions are usually a thick, approximately 7 inches, round, whereas those cooked in restaurants or homes are thinner and smaller.

MAKES ABOUT 8 PANCAKES

I cup less 2 tablespoons whole mung beans, soaked for 10 hours

2 tablespoons short-grain rice, washed and soaked (see page 102)

½ cup diced red bell pepper

I garlic clove, crushed and finely chopped

½ onion, diced

2 scallions, white and some green parts sliced

I tablespoon Crushed Toasted Sesame Seeds (see page 22)

2 teaspoons sesame oil

I tablespoon soy sauce

6 ounces mung bean sprouts

vegetable oil for frying

Seasoned Dipping Sauce (see page 75) to serve

❖ Rub the beans, without draining them, between your palms to detach the skin. Pour off the water, which will take a lot of the skins with it. Cover the beans again and repeat the process until all the skins have been removed. Put the beans into a blender or food processor.

❖ Drain the rice and add to the blender or food processor with 4 tablespoons water. Mix to a paste, then, with the motor running, slowly pour in ½ cup water. Pour into a bowl and stir in the red bell pepper, garlic, onion, scallions, sesame seeds, sesame oil and soy sauce.

❖ Add the mung bean sprouts to a saucepan of boiling water. Cover and quickly return to a boil. Boil for 2 minutes, then drain and squeeze out as much water as possible. Separate the bean sprouts and stir into the batter.

❖ Heat a little oil in a skillet, preferably nonstick. Stir the batter and add a ladleful to the pan, spreading it out evenly with the back of the ladle. Trickle 1 teaspoon vegetable oil over the top of the pancake. Cover the pan and cook the pancake for 2½–3 minutes.

❖ Turn the pancake over and cook, uncovered, for 2½–3 minutes more.

❖ Slide the pancake onto a warmed plate and cook the remaining batter in the same way.

SCALLION PANCAKES

Pajon I

These delicious pancakes are one of Korea's national dishes (rather confusingly they are known as "Korean pizzas;" they bear only a tenuous resemblance to Italian pizzas). They are served straight from the sizzling pan, cut into squares so they can be picked up easily with chopsticks.

SERVES 3-4

¾ cup all-purpose flour

¾ cup rice flour

salt

I large egg, beaten

I teaspoon sesame oil

3 tablespoons vegetable oil

6 scallions, quartered lengthways, each length
   cut into 3-inch long strips

Vinegar Dipping Sauce (see page 32) to serve

◀ *Scallion Pancakes (right) and*
Scallion and Shrimp Pancakes

❖ Stir together the flours and salt. Stir in the egg, then slowly pour in 1 cup water, stirring, to make a smooth batter. Stir in the sesame oil. Leave for 30 minutes.

❖ Heat 1 tablespoon vegetable oil in an 8-inch nonstick skillet over a medium-low heat. Sprinkle one third of the scallions evenly over the bottom, then pour over one-third of the batter. Cover and cook for 5–6 minutes. Turn the pancake, cover again and cook for 3 minutes more. Remove the lid and cook for another 2 minutes. Transfer to a warm plate and repeat. Cut the pancakes into 2-inch squares and serve hot with the Vinegar Dipping Sauce.

SCALLION AND SHRIMP PANCAKES
Pajon 2

This is a more elaborate version of the previous recipe. Break and lightly beat the eggs as you need them.

SERVES 4-6

I cup all-purpose flour

I cup rice flour

salt and freshly ground black pepper

about 5 eggs

2 teaspoons sesame oil

dash of soy sauce

vegetable oil for frying

10 large scallions, white and some green parts
   split lengthways and cut into strips

I red bell pepper, cut into strips

I zucchini, cut into strips

I cup cooked, shelled shrimp

Ginger Dipping Sauce (see page 35) to serve

❖ Season the flours, then stir in two of the eggs, the sesame oil and soy sauce. Slowly pour in about ⅔ cup water, stirring, to make a medium-thick batter. Leave for 30 minutes.

❖ Heat a very fine layer of vegetable oil in a large skillet, preferably nonstick. Pour in one-third of the batter. Scatter over one-third of the scallions, pepper, zucchini and shrimp. Cook over a medium-hot heat for 5–7 minutes until set and browned underneath. Carefully turn over the pancake and cook for 5–7 minutes more.

❖ Cook the remaining batter, vegetables, shrimp and eggs in the same way. Serve, cut into squares, with Ginger Dipping Sauce.

NINE-SECTION APPETIZER

Kujolpan

Traditionally, small pancakes are served in a pile surrounded by a ring of eight fillings, all in their own lacquered dish. Each person takes a pancake and fills it with whichever filling they like, then rolls it up with their fingers. Kijolpan is great for relaxed leisurely eating with friends whether you serve it as a first course or a snack. The fillings should all look different and provide a variety of tastes and textures. This recipe may look complicated, but each of the fillings is very quick and easy to prepare. A *kimchi* (see pages 40–64) could be used in place of one of the fillings.

SERVES 4-6

1 cup all-purpose flour
salt and freshly ground black
 pepper
vegetable oil for frying

CUCUMBER FILLING
salt
½ cucumber, sliced into thin
 strips
2 teaspoons sesame oil

MUSHROOM FILLING
6 shiitake mushrooms, sliced
2–3 teaspoons sesame oil
1 teaspoon soy sauce
freshly ground black pepper

MEAT FILLING
4 ounces sirloin or rump
 steak, cut into very fine
 strips
1 small garlic clove, crushed
 and finely chopped
1 scallion, white part and a
 little green part, finely
 chopped
1 tablespoon soy sauce
1 teaspoon Crushed Toasted
 Sesame Seeds (see page 22)
freshly ground black pepper
1½–2 teaspoons sesame oil

BAMBOO SHOOT FILLING
4 ounces bamboo shoots, cut
 into fine strips
½-inch piece of fresh ginger,
 cut into very fine strips
1½ teaspoons soy sauce
1 teaspoon sesame oil

EGG FILLING
2 eggs
salt and freshly ground black
 pepper
vegetable oil for frying

CARROT FILLING

I carrot, cut into very fine
 strips
I teaspoon rice vinegar
I teaspoon sugar

SHRIMP FILLING

I cup chopped, cooked, shelled
 shrimp
I ½ teaspoons rice vinegar
pinch of Korean chili pepper,
 or cayenne pepper mixed
 with paprika
salt

❖ To make the pancakes, sift the flour and seasoning into a bowl, then slowly pour in about ¾ cup water to make a smooth batter. Leave for 30 minutes.

❖ Heat a very shallow layer of oil in a skillet. Add spoonfuls of the batter and spread out to form 3-inch diameter rounds. Fry until lightly browned on both sides. Stack in piles in a small, shallow round serving dish.

❖ To make the cucumber filling, put the cucumber in a colander. Sprinkle with salt and leave for 30 minutes. Rinse well and squeeze out as much water as possible. Heat the sesame oil in a skillet and fry the cucumber for 2–3 minutes. Transfer to a small serving dish.

❖ To make the mushroom filling, heat the oil in a skillet. Add the mushrooms and stir-fry for 3–4 minutes. Toss with the soy sauce and transfer to a small serving dish.

❖ To make the meat filling, mix the beef with the garlic, scallion, soy sauce, sesame seeds and pepper. Heat the sesame oil in a skillet. Add the beef mixture and stir-fry for 4–5 minutes. Transfer to a small serving dish.

❖ To make the bamboo shoot filling, mix the bamboo shoots with the ginger and soy sauce. Heat the sesame oil in a skillet and stir-fry the bamboo shoots for 2–3 minutes. Transfer to a small serving dish.

❖ To make the egg filling, lightly beat the yolks and the whites with the seasoning. Heat the oil in a skillet. Fry the egg to make an "omelet" and cut into strips (see page 85). Transfer to a small serving dish.

❖ To make the carrot filling, mix all the ingredients together. Transfer to a small serving dish.

❖ To make the shrimp filling, mix all the ingredients together. Transfer to a small serving dish.

❖ To assemble the appetizer, put the dish of pancakes in the center and arrange the other dishes in a ring around it.

BROILED PORK BELLY

Samgyopsalgui

Samgyopsalgui are rather like a Korean version of Spanish *tapas* because they are served to customers in city *suljip* (or drinking houses) in order to increase thirst and therefore drink sales. Plates of thinly sliced, rolled belly of pork are given to customers, who cook it themselves on table-top burners and then dip the crisp, slightly charred, morsels in a simple sesame oil and salt dip.

SERVES 6

1 pound belly of pork, thinly sliced

about 4 tablespoons sesame oil

2 teaspoons sea salt

❖ Preheat the broiler or barbecue, or use a table-top burner. Stir together the sesame oil and salt in a small serving bowl.

❖ Cook the pork slices until crisp and slightly charred. Drain quickly on paper towels and serve hot with the dip. Don't forget to offer plenty of paper napkins.

CRISP KELP

Tasima

Tasima is the Korean name for kelp, which is more widely known by the Japanese name of *konbu*, also spelled *kombu*. It is sold in thick slices and is available from ethnic and healthfood stores. When deep-fried like this so that it is crisp on the outside yet chewy to eat, it is a favorite "nibble" with drinks. Do not wash the *tasima* but wipe it just before frying.

SERVES 4

vegetable oil for deep-frying

2 tablespoons sesame oil

**about 3 ounces *tasima*, cut into 1½-inch long
   strips**

sugar for sprinkling (optional)

❖ Half fill a deep-fat fryer with vegetable oil and add the sesame oil. Heat it to 350°F. Add the *tasima* in batches if necessary, so the pan is not crowded, and fry for about 10 seconds until the surface blisters and crackles; do not let it burn. Transfer to paper towels to drain. Serve hot, sprinkled with a little sugar, if liked.

KOREAN STEAK TARTARE

Yukhoe

Yukhoe is similar to steak tartare but there are important differences – whereas *filet mignon* is used for steak tartare, round steak is considered better for Yukhoe. Yukhoe is also more highly seasoned.

SERVES 4

1 pound piece of round steak, frozen for 1 hour
1 tablespoon rice wine or dry sherry
3 tablespoons soy sauce
1 tablespoon sesame oil
1 tablespoon Crushed Toasted Sesame Seeds
    (see page 22)
1 tablespoon sugar
2½ garlic cloves, crushed and finely chopped
½-inch piece of fresh ginger, finely chopped
freshly ground black pepper
scallions, white and green part thinly sliced on
    the diagonal
toasted sesame seeds to garnish

❖ Using a very sharp knife, cut the beef across the grain into wafer-thin slices. Pile the slices into stacks and cut across into very fine matchsticks. Put into a large bowl.

❖ Add the rice wine or dry sherry, soy sauce, sesame oil and sesame seeds, sugar, garlic, ginger and plenty of pepper. Mix gently but thoroughly – in Korea this would be done with the hands. Form into a loose ball, cover and chill for 1–2 hours.

❖ Using your hands, mound the beef on a cold serving plate, and garnish with scallions and toasted sesame seeds.

SESAME-GRILLED SEAWEED

Kimgui

Crisp, smoky, nutty-tasting, paper-thin sheets of grilled *kim* or laver (also known as *nori*) are an extremely moreish "nibble" to serve with drinks.

SERVES ABOUT 4

8–10 sheets *kim* (laver or *nori*)
sesame oil for brushing
salt
toasted sesame seeds to serve

❖ Brush both sides of each sheet of *kim* with sesame oil and sprinkle with salt.

❖ Hold each sheet in turn in tongs and pass backward and forward over a fairly low gas flame until crisp.

❖ Sprinkle the *kim* sheets with toasted sesame seeds. Let people break off pieces as they like, or cut the sheets into strips or squares.

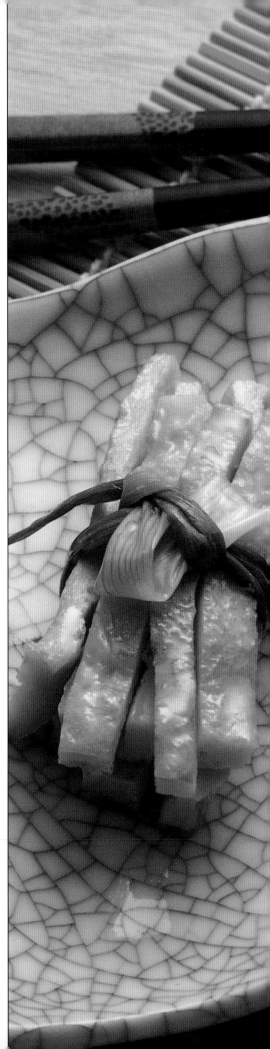

EGG STRIP BUNDLES

Chon

Egg strips are tied in bundles with "strings" of blanched scallion. In Korea the eggs are cooked in rectangular pans; as these are difficult to find elsewhere, you can use an ordinary round crêpe pan or skillet and trim the curves of the "omelets". Serve with whichever dipping sauce you like, or even a selection of them.

SERVES 4-6

5 eggs
salt and freshly ground black pepper
12 scallions, trimmed
vegetable oil for frying
Dipping Sauce of choice (see vinegar page 32,
   sesame page 58, and ginger page 35) to serve

❖ Lightly beat the eggs with the seasoning.

❖ Heat a very fine layer of oil in a 6-inch skillet, preferably nonstick. Pour in half of the eggs. Cover and cook over a low heat for 5–6 minutes until the bottom of the "omelet" is firm. Using a spatula, turn the "omelet" over and cook for 2–3 minutes more until the second side is firm. Remove and let cool. Cook the remaining egg in the same way.

❖ Lower the scallions, bulbs first, into a saucepan of boiling water, easing in the green parts as they soften. Cover and quickly return to a boil. Boil for 2 minutes, then drain and rinse under running cold water. Dry on paper towels. Split each scallion lengthways into two or more strands by cutting through the bulb, then tearing upward.

❖ Trim the curves of the "omelets," then cut the "omelets" into strips about 2½ inches long by ¼ inch wide.

❖ Make bundles of eight to ten egg strips each. Wrap a strip of scallion around the center of each bundle and tuck the end of the scallion under the binding. Arrange the bundles on a serving plate and serve with a dipping sauce.

STUFFED CHILIES

Kochujon

Touching chilies can make your hands, particularly any cuts or bruises, sting so it is a good idea to wear fine rubber gloves when preparing this dish. Serve Kochujon as a first course.

SERVES 4

2 cups freshly ground lean pork

I garlic clove, finely chopped

½-inch piece of fresh ginger, finely chopped

4 scallions, finely chopped

2 teaspoons Crushed Toasted Sesame Seeds
  (see page 22)

2–3 teaspoons soy sauce

16–20 large fresh red chilies

seasoned all-purpose flour for coating

I large egg, beaten

vegetable oil for frying

Vinegar Dipping Sauce (see below) to serve

❖ Mix the pork, garlic, ginger, scallions, sesame seeds and soy sauce together very well.

❖ Cut the chilies in half lengthways and remove the seeds. Break off small pieces of the meat mixture to fill the chilies. Form into torpedo shapes and use to stuff the chilies, packing the meat stuffing in firmly.

❖ Roll the stuffed chilies in seasoned flour to give an even coating, then dip in beaten egg.

❖ Heat a ½-inch layer of oil in a skillet. Add the chilies in batches and fry for 4–5 minutes on each side until golden brown and cooked through. Remove from the oil with a slotted spoon and drain on paper towels. Serve hot with Vinegar Dipping Sauce.

VINEGAR DIPPING SAUCE

Chojang I

This can serve as a basic Korean dipping sauce.

MAKES 10 TBSP

7 tablespoons soy sauce

2 tablespoons rice vinegar

½-inch piece of fresh ginger, grated

2 teaspoons Crushed Toasted Sesame Seeds

about ½ teaspoon Korean chili powder

pinch of sugar

❖ Combine the soy sauce and vinegar in a small bowl, and add remaining ingredients. If you do not have the chili powder, use cayenne pepper mixed with paprika.

Stuffed Chilies ▶

KOREAN CRAB CAKES

Kejon

Although not quite authentic, I like to serve Kejon with a crisp green salad.

SERVES 4

12 ounces floury potatoes, unpeeled
1½ garlic cloves, crushed and finely chopped
1 fresh red chili, seeded and finely chopped
1-inch piece of fresh ginger, grated
3 scallions, finely chopped
1½ cups white and brown crab meat
finely grated rind of ½ lime
2 tablespoons chopped fresh cilantro
salt and freshly ground black pepper
1½ tablespoons sesame seeds
1 cup fresh bread crumbs, for coating
flour for coating
1 egg, beaten
vegetable oil for deep-frying
Ginger Dipping Sauce (see below) to serve

◀ *Korean Crab Cakes*

❖ Boil the potatoes in their skins until tender. Drain and leave until cool enough to handle. Peel the potatoes and mash the flesh.

❖ Mix the mashed potato with the garlic, chili, ginger, scallions, crab meat, lime zest, cilantro and salt and pepper. Form into eight round cakes about the size of golf balls. Chill for 30 minutes.

❖ Stir the sesame seeds into the bread crumbs. Coat the crab cakes in the flour, then the egg and finally coat in the bread crumbs, pressing in the crumbs firmly.

❖ Half fill a deep-fat fryer with vegetable oil and heat to about 325°F. Fry the crab cakes in batches for about 8 minutes until golden. Transfer to paper towels to drain while frying the remaining crab cakes. Serve hot with Ginger Dipping Sauce.

GINGER DIPPING SAUCE

Chojang 2

There are no chilies in this sauce but ginger provides some "hotness."
Also the predominance of soy sauce and rice vinegar are reversed.

MAKES ABOUT 10 TABLESPOONS

6 tablespoons rice vinegar
1-inch piece of fresh ginger, grated
2 scallions, white part only, finely chopped
2 tablespoons dark soy sauce
2 teaspoons sugar

❖ Pour the vinegar into a small bowl. Add the remaining ingredients and mix together well.

OYSTER FRITTERS

Kulwigim

Use Pacific oysters for these fritters – not only are they the authentic ones, but they may be cheaper than those grown off the east coast such as bluepoint. Save the liquid that is in the oyster shells to strain into the batter; reduce the water by the amount of oyster liquid added and omit the salt from the recipe if you do this.

Add some sesame seeds to the batter if liked, for an extra nutty, crunchy texture.

SERVES 4-6

I cup all-purpose flour

2 teaspoons baking powder

very small pinch of Korean chili powder,
   or cayenne pepper mixed with paprika

salt

I egg, beaten

about 24 oysters, opened

vegetable oil for deep-frying

Sesame or Vinegar Dipping Sauce (see pages 58
   and 32) to serve

❖ Sift the flour, baking powder, Korean chili powder, or cayenne pepper and paprika, and salt into a bowl. Slowly pour in ⅔ cup water, stirring, to make a smooth batter. Leave for 30 minutes.

❖ Half fill a deep-fat fryer with vegetable oil and heat to about 350°F. Dip the oysters in the batter, then fry for about 2 minutes until the batter is crisp and golden; take care not to overcook the oysters as they will become tough.

❖ Drain the oysters on paper towels and serve hot with Sesame or Vinegar Dipping Sauce.

ABOVE *Fishing is prevalent in Korea, providing
a wealth of fish, shellfish and sea vegetables.*

CRISPY ANCHOVIES

Marunmyolchi

The dried anchovies for this dish are about the size of European whitebait and are deep-fried in the same way. They can be found in most Japanese supermarkets. If the anchovies are very salty, rub or rinse off excess salt before frying. Deep-fried anchovies mixed with a sweet/hot sauce which contrast with their saltiness, are extremely moreish.

SERVES 4

1 garlic clove, finely chopped
1 small onion, chopped
1 fresh red chili, seeded
¾ teaspoon salt
1½ teaspoons sugar
2 tablespoons vegetable oil, plus extra for deep-
    frying
about 4 ounces dried anchovies, heads removed if
    liked, rinsed if necessary
fresh cilantro leaves for garnish

❖ Grind the garlic, onion and chili to a paste with the salt. Mix in the sugar. Set aside.

❖ Heat the 2 tablespoons vegetable oil in a skillet. Add the onion paste and cook, stirring occasionally, for 3–4 minutes. Meanwhile, half fill a deep-fat fryer with vegetable oil and heat to 350°F. Add the anchovies so the pan is not crowded (in batches if necessary), and fry for 20–30 seconds until very crisp and lightly colored.

❖ Transfer the anchovies to paper towels to drain, then tip into the skillet and heat through, shaking the pan. Pour into a serving bowl and garnish with cilantro leaves.

STEAMED PORK AND SHRIMP CUSTARD

Altchim

For this pork- and shrimp-packed custard you will need a shallow flameproof dish that will fit inside a steaming basket. Alternatively, the mixture may be steamed in four individual dishes for 12–15 minutes.

SERVES 4

1 cup lean ground pork

1 tablespoon soy sauce

1 teaspoon sesame oil

1 garlic clove, crushed and finely chopped

¼-inch piece of fresh ginger, grated

4 eggs

1 teaspoon toasted sesame seeds

½ cup cooked, shelled shrimp

2 scallions, white part and a little green part finely chopped

freshly ground black pepper

◆ Mix together the pork, soy sauce, sesame oil, garlic and ginger. Transfer to a shallow flameproof dish and fry, stirring to break up the pork, until the pork has changed color.

◆ Beat the eggs with a little water.

◆ Remove the dish from the heat and stir in the eggs, sesame seeds, shrimp, scallions and pepper. Cover with baking parchment and place in a steaming basket. Put the steaming basket over a saucepan of boiling water and steam for 17–20 minutes until the custard is just set in the center.

SALADS, VEGETABLES AND PICKLED VEGETABLES

Korean salads, often made from lightly steamed or fried vegetables, are simply and lightly dressed with soy sauce, sesame oil and rice vinegar, and usually flavored with the characteristic flavorings – garlic, ginger, scallions and chili.

A selection of salads and vegetables are served as part of the *panchan* (side dishes) that accompany Korean meals. Pickled vegetables, *kimchis* in particular, are a Korean passion and no cook worth their salt would serve a proper meal without at least one *kimchi*.

SPINACH SALAD

Shigumchinamul

This salad is equally good served warm or chilled.

SERVES 4

1 pound young fresh spinach leaves
1 garlic clove, crushed and finely chopped
1 tablespoon sesame oil
2 tablespoons soy sauce
2 teaspoons sesame seeds
freshly ground black pepper

◆ Add the spinach to a large saucepan of boiling water. Cover and quickly return to a boil. Boil for 1 minute, then tip the spinach into a colander and refresh under running cold water. Drain, then dry on paper towels.

◆ Coarsely shred the spinach, then toss with the remaining ingredients. Serve warm, or leave until cold, then cover and chill. Toss again before serving.

BEAN SPROUT SALAD

Kongnamul

This is a much loved, crunchy, nutritious salad or side dish. In restaurants it may be served with your pre-prandial drinks, so you have something to nibble while you are waiting for your meal to arrive.

SERVES 4-6

1½ pounds soybean sprouts or mung bean
  sprouts
2 garlic cloves, very finely chopped
5 scallions, white and green parts thinly sliced
  into rings
1 fresh hot red chili, seeded and thinly sliced into
  rings
1 tablespoon Crushed Toasted Sesame Seeds
  (see page 22)
salt

◆ Remove the roots from the bean sprouts. Add the bean sprouts to a pan of boiling water. Return to a boil, then tip into a colander and rinse under running cold water. Squeeze as much water as possible from the bean sprouts.

◆ Toss the bean sprouts with the remaining ingredients. Serve at room temperature or slightly chilled.

Bean Sprout Salad (left) and Spinach Salad ▶

WHITE RADISH PICKLE

Kakdooki

Some people find that chilies and chili powder irritate their skin; if this happens to you, wear fine rubber gloves when rubbing the chili powder into the radish.

FILLS A JAR

2 tablespoons Korean chili powder or cayenne
   pepper mixed with paprika
1¾ pounds white radish, cut into 1-inch cubes
4 scallions, white and green parts thinly sliced
1-inch piece of fresh ginger, finely chopped
1 small garlic clove, finely chopped
2 teaspoons sugar
4 teaspoons salt

❖ Rub the chili powder or cayenne and paprika into the white radish. Put in a bowl and leave for 30 minutes.

❖ Mix the remaining ingredients with the white radish, and cover with plastic wrap. Put a plate that just fits inside the bowl, on top of the plastic wrap, and put a heavy weight on top. Leave for about 48 hours until the liquid rises above the white radish.

❖ Remove the weight and leave the pickle for 3–7 days, depending on the temperature, until it turns sour.

❖ Transfer the pickle to a dry, clean jar. Cover with a vinegar-proof lid and keep in a cold, dark place. It will keep for up to a year in these conditions.

ABOVE *Local food markets with hustle and bustle and a warm atmosphere are a common sight throughout Korea.*

WHITE RADISH SALAD

Muusaengchae I

In Korea, they use long, pointed white radishes that are known in the West by the Japanese name of *daikon* or the Indian name of *mooli*. They are available in some markets as well as ethnic stores.

SERVES 3-4

1 white radish, coarsely grated or cut
    lengthways into fine strips
salt
½–1 teaspoon Korean chili powder, or cayenne
    pepper mixed with paprika
2 teaspoons sugar
1 tablespoon sesame oil
4 tablespoons rice vinegar
½-inch piece of fresh ginger, finely chopped
sesame seeds for garnish

❖ Put the white radish into a colander. Mix with salt and leave for 10–15 minutes.

❖ Rinse the radish well, then drain and dry thoroughly on paper towels.

❖ Toss the radish with the remaining ingredients, except the sesame seeds. Cover and chill. Garnish with sesame seeds to serve.

CUCUMBER SALAD

Oinamul

Mixing the cucumber with salt and leaving it for 1 hour draws out moisture, so preventing the sauce from being watery.

SERVES 2-4

1 long cucumber, very thinly sliced
salt
pinch of Korean chili powder, or cayenne pepper
    mixed with paprika
1 tablespoon sugar
2 tablespoons rice vinegar
sesame oil for sprinkling

❖ Put the cucumber slices in a bowl. Toss with salt, then add cold water to cover. Leave for 1 hour. Drain the cucumber. If the cucumber tastes very salty, rinse it under running cold water and dry thoroughly on paper towels. Put the cucumber into a bowl.

❖ Mix the Korean chili powder, or cayenne pepper and paprika, with the sugar and vinegar, and pour over the cucumber. Sprinkle with sesame oil and toss to mix. Cover and chill. Toss again before serving.

EGGPLANT SALAD WITH SESAME SEEDS

Khajinamul

Khajinamul doubles as a salad and a first course; it is usually served at the beginning of a meal, then left on the table until the end.

SERVES 4-6

1 ¼ pounds oriental eggplants, or small,
    slim eggplants
1 scallion, white and green part sliced
    into rings
1 tablespoon sugar
1 tablespoon sesame oil
3 tablespoons Japanese soy sauce
2 garlic cloves, finely chopped
2 tablespoons rice vinegar
2 tablespoons Crushed Toasted Sesame
    Seeds (see page 22)
salt

❖ If using oriental eggplants, cut them lengthways into quarters, then slice across the middle of each piece. If using ordinary eggplants, cut them into long pieces about 1 inch thick and 1 inch wide.

❖ Steam the pieces of eggplant in a covered container until tender and soft.

❖ Meanwhile, mix together the remaining ingredients.

❖ Leave the eggplants until cool enough to handle, then tear into long, thin strips. Put into a bowl. Pour over the dressing mixture and stir together. Serve at room temperature, or chill before serving.

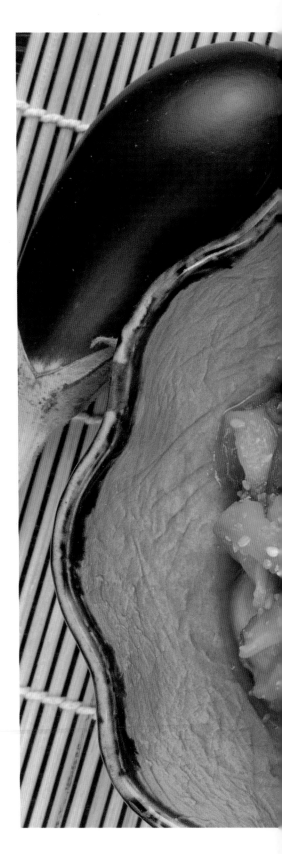

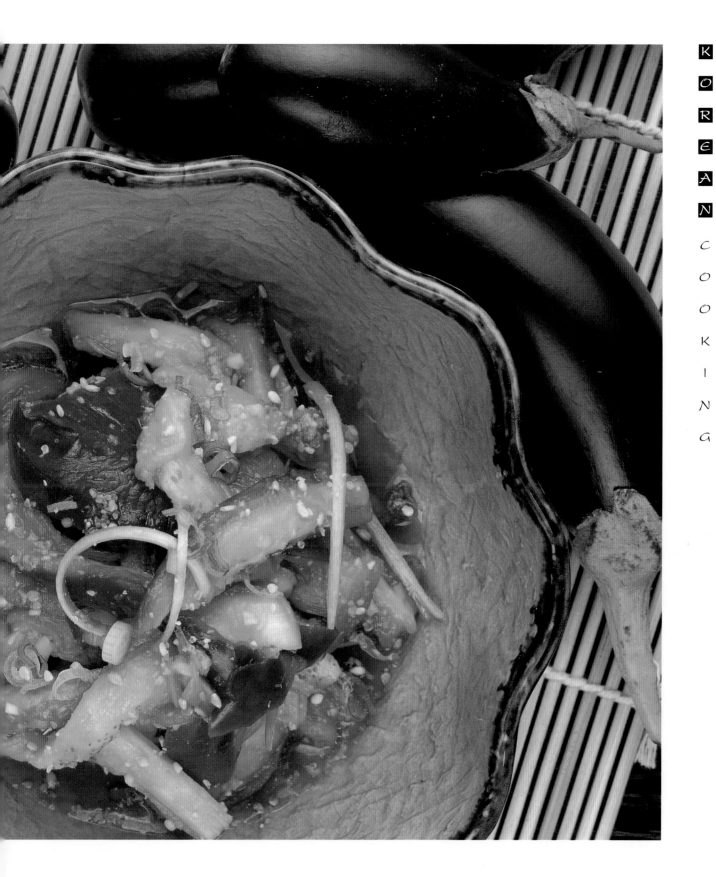

LOTUS ROOT SALAD

Namul

Lotus roots have a firm, crunchy texture, a taste similar to artichoke hearts, and the slices display an attractive flower-like pattern.

SERVES 2-4

4 ounces young lotus roots, thinly sliced

2 tablespoons soy sauce

I tablespoon rice vinegar

2 teaspoons sesame oil

2 teaspoons toasted sesame seeds

I teaspoon sugar

❖ Arrange the lotus roots in a steaming basket. Cover and put over a saucepan of boiling water. Steam for about 1 hour – the time will depend on the age and therefore toughness of the roots.

❖ Transfer the lotus roots to a bowl. Add the remaining ingredients and stir together. Serve warm or chilled.

CARROT AND WHITE RADISH SALAD

Mou Sangchae

Both the colors and flavors of white radish and carrot complement each other in this attractive salad.

SERVES 4

I carrot, thinly sliced on the diagonal

8 ounces white radish, cut into fine strips

salt

I tablespoon sesame oil

I teaspoon soy sauce

I teaspoon sugar

very small pinch of Korean chili powder,
  or cayenne pepper mixed with paprika

❖ Cut the carrot slices into very fine strips and put into a bowl with the white radish strips. Sprinkle lightly with salt, and toss together well; then leave for 1 hour. Drain, then rinse and drain thoroughly, pressing out as much liquid as possible. Dry on paper towels.

❖ Mix the vegetables with the remaining ingredients and serve.

◀ *Carrot and White Radish Salad (above)*
and Lotus Root Salad

MUSHROOMS BAKED IN FOIL
Posot

Cooking mushrooms in foil so the aroma, flavor and juices are trapped inside is a specialty of many of Korea's older, traditional restaurants. The unseasoned mushrooms are either eaten plain, with a dipping sauce or as a contrast to hot and garlicky dishes.

SERVES 2-4

6 ounces large white mushrooms, caps and stalks
   cut into ¼-inch slices
Vinegar Dipping Sauce (see page 32) (optional)

❖ Cut a large piece of foil – about 20 by 12 inches. Put the mushrooms in the center of the foil. Fold over the long sides of the foil, then the short sides to make a neat, secure package.

❖ Preheat a barbecue or broiler. Cook the mushroom packages about 4 inches from the heat for 5–7 minutes.

❖ Serve the mushrooms straightaway, accompanied by a dipping sauce if liked.

COOKED WATERCRESS SALAD
Minarinamul

Steaming the watercress rather than boiling it keeps it drier and saves having to drain it.

SERVES 4

2 large bunches watercress
3 tablespoons soy sauce
1 tablespoon sesame oil
2 teaspoons toasted sesame seeds
salt and freshly ground black pepper

❖ Cut off and discard the coarse parts of the watercress stalks, then spread it out in a shallow layer in a steaming basket; you may have to cook the watercress in two batches if the steaming basket is not very large. Cover the basket and put over a saucepan of boiling water. Steam for 1–2 minutes. Remove the watercress from the steaming basket and coarsely chop it.

❖ Toss the watercress with the soy sauce, sesame oil and seeds, salt and pepper. Leave until cold, then cover and chill. Toss again before serving.

MUSHROOMS WITH CHICKEN AND VEGETABLES

Posotbokkum

Mushrooms of many different types are very popular in Korea. The most widely available of these in the West are both fresh and dried shiitake (when dried they are more commonly known as dried Chinese black mushrooms), dried wood ear (also known as cloud ear and tree ear), which have little flavor but a pleasing texture and attractive appearance, and stone mushrooms.

SERVES 3-4

6 ounces chicken breast, cut into strips

3 garlic cloves, crushed and finely chopped

4 tablespoons soy sauce

2 teaspoons sesame oil

freshly ground black pepper

vegetable oil for frying

1 pound shiitake or oyster mushrooms, thinly sliced

1 red bell pepper, cut into thin strips

1 zucchini, thinly sliced diagonally

4 scallions, white and some green parts thinly sliced diagonally

fresh cilantro leaves for garnish

❖ Mix the chicken with the garlic, soy sauce, sesame oil and plenty of black pepper. Leave for 30 minutes.

❖ Heat a little vegetable oil in a large skillet. Lift the chicken from the marinade (reserve the marinade) and stir-fry for 2 minutes or so.

❖ Stir in all the vegetables and cook, stirring, for about 5 minutes until the vegetables are tender but still crisp. Stir in the reserved marinade about 1 minute before the end of cooking. Serve garnished with cilantro leaves.

ABOVE *Mount Chirisan in Spring. A National Park, famous for outstanding beauty and superb hiking.*

STIR-FRY PORK AND VEGETABLE SALAD

Twaepyon

The vegetables can be altered according to taste
or availability.

SERVES 4

vegetable oil for frying

4-ounce piece of pork loin, cut
   into fine strips

1 small turnip, cut into 2-inch
   long strips

1 small carrot, cut into 2-inch
   long strips

1 small onion, cut into 2-inch
   long strips

2–3 celery stalks, cut into
   2-inch long strips

2 ounces mushroom caps, cut
   into 2-inch long strips

1 small garlic clove, crushed
   and finely chopped

1 teaspoon grated fresh ginger

2 scallions, white and some
   green parts finely chopped

3 tablespoons soy sauce

1 ½ teaspoons sesame oil

1 tablespoon sugar

1 teaspoon rice vinegar

freshly ground black pepper

sesame seeds for garnish

❖ Heat about 2 tablespoons of oil in a skillet. Add the pork and
stir-fry for 3–4 minutes until cooked through. Using a slotted
spoon, transfer it to a bowl.

❖ Add the turnip and carrot strips to the pan and fry for 5–7
minutes until just beginning to soften.

❖ Add the onion and celery to a saucepan of boiling water and
simmer for 2–3 minutes. Drain and refresh under running cold
water. Add to the pork with the mushrooms, garlic, ginger and
scallions.

❖ Using a slotted spoon, transfer the turnips and carrots to paper
towels to drain.

❖ Whisk together the soy sauce, sesame oil, sugar and rice
vinegar. Add the turnips and carrots to the pork. Pour over the
dressing and toss. Leave until cold. Serve sprinkled with sesame
seeds.

SPICED WHITE RADISH SALAD

Muusaengchae 2

White radishes have a milder flavor than Western red radishes, so respond well to being mixed with typical Korean flavorings.

SERVES 4

I large white radish, sliced

salt

I tablespoon soy sauce

2 teaspoons rice vinegar

½-inch piece of fresh ginger, finely chopped

I teaspoon sugar

2 teaspoons Crushed Toasted Sesame Seeds
   (see page 22)

I ½ teaspoons *kochujang* (see page 69) or chili
   bean paste

I garlic clove, finely chopped

I scallion, white and green part thinly sliced
   diagonally

❖ Put the white radish into a colander, mix with salt and leave for 10–15 minutes.

❖ Rinse the radish well, then drain and dry thoroughly on paper towels.

❖ Mix together the remaining ingredients, except the scallions, and toss with the white radish. Scatter over the scallions, cover and chill. Toss lightly before serving.

◀ *Soy-Glazed Pumpkin*

SOY-GLAZED PUMPKIN

Yachaejorim

The mixture of pumpkin with ginger and soy sauce gives attractive color, taste and texture combinations.

SERVES 4

8 ounces pumpkin, cut into I-inch cubes

½ cup sugar

2-inch piece of fresh ginger, grated

6 tablespoons soy sauce

freshly ground black pepper

toasted sesame seeds and garlic chives
   for garnish

❖ Cook the pumpkin in boiling water for 2 minutes. Drain well, then put into a skillet. Add 6 tablespoons of water, the sugar, ginger, soy sauce and pepper. Heat slowly, stirring carefully, until the sugar dissolves. Then partially cover and simmer slowly for about 15 minutes, stirring occasionally, until the pumpkin is tender and glazed with soy syrup.

❖ Garnish with sesame seeds and garlic chives.

ZUCCHINI WITH BEEF

Hobakmuchim

Hobakmuchim is a simple but very tasty dish that can be served in
traditional Korean manner with *kimchis*, rice, salads and vegetables,
or Western-style with a green vegetable or salad.

SERVES 2-4

4 small zucchini, cut diagonally into ¼-inch thick
 slices
salt
1 cup freshly ground, lean beef
2 tablespoons vegetable oil
2 scallions, white and green parts very thinly
 sliced
1 tablespoon sugar
1 tablespoon soy sauce
½–1 teaspoon chili powder
toasted sesame seeds for garnish

MARINADE

1 scallion, white and green part very thinly sliced
2 garlic cloves, crushed and finely chopped
1½ tablespoons soy sauce
1 tablespoon sesame oil
1-inch piece of fresh ginger, finely chopped
1 tablespoon toasted sesame seeds
freshly ground black pepper

❖ Put the zucchini in a colander, and sprinkle
generously with salt. Toss together and leave for
30 minutes. Meanwhile, mix all the marinade
ingredients together. Add the ground beef, and
leave for 30 minutes.

❖ Rinse the zucchini well and dry thoroughly
with paper towels. Heat the vegetable oil in a
large skillet over a fairly high heat. Add the beef
and marinade, and fry, stirring to break up the
lumps, for about 1 minute or until the beef
changes color.

❖ Lightly stir in the zucchini, then add the
remaining ingredients, except the sesame seeds.
Cook for 2 minutes, stirring lightly. Lower the
heat and continue to stir for another minute
until the zucchini are tender but still retain
some bite.

❖ Serve sprinkled with toasted sesame seeds.

FRIED ZUCCHINI WITH SESAME SEEDS

Hobakjon

A coating of sesame seeds gives zucchini an interesting nutty flavor and crunchy/crisp texture.

SERVES 4

1¼ pounds small zucchini, cut diagonally into
   ¼-inch thick slices
salt
seasoned all-purpose flour for coating
1 large egg, beaten
sesame seeds for coating
vegetable oil for frying
Sesame Dipping Sauce (see page 58) or Vinegar
   Dipping Sauce (see page 32) to serve

*(clockwise from left) Fried Zucchini
with Sesame Seeds, Carrot Fritters,
and Deep-Fried Eggplants (p58)* ▶

❖ Put the zucchini into a colander. Toss generously with salt and leave for 30 minutes.

❖ Rinse the zucchini well and dry thoroughly with paper towels. Toss the zucchini in seasoned all-purpose flour to coat evenly, then dip in beaten egg. Finally, coat in sesame seeds.

❖ Heat a thin layer of oil in a wide skillet. Add the zucchini slices in a single layer and fry for 3–4 minutes on each side until golden on the outside but still crisp on the inside.

❖ Using a slotted spoon, transfer to paper towels to drain. Serve hot with Sesame or Vinegar Dipping Sauce.

CARROT FRITTERS

Hobak

Any of the dipping sauces in this book can be served to accompany these carrot slices.

SERVES 2-4

2 carrots, thinly sliced diagonally
4 tablespoons all-purpose flour
1 large egg, beaten
vegetable oil for frying
Sesame Dipping Sauce (see page 58)

❖ Coat the carrot slices lightly and evenly in the flour, then dip in beaten egg.

❖ Heat a ¼-inch layer of oil in a skillet. Add the carrot slices and fry in a single layer until golden brown on both sides. Using a slotted spoon, transfer the carrot slices to paper towels to drain. Serve hot with a dipping sauce.

DEEP-FRIED EGGPLANTS

Kajijon

Jon is the name given to ingredients that are coated in flour, then dipped in egg and fried. These eggplant *jon* can be served as a first course, or to eat with drinks; in which case, supply toothpicks for spearing the eggplant slices.

SERVES 4

2 eggplants, thinly sliced on the diagonal
salt
all-purpose flour for coating
Korean chili powder, or cayenne pepper
  mixed with paprika
1–1½ tablespoons chopped fresh cilantro
1 large egg, beaten
oil for deep-frying
Sesame Dipping Sauce (see below) to serve

❖ Put the eggplant slices into a colander. Toss with salt and leave for 30 minutes. Rinse the eggplant slices, drain and dry thoroughly on paper towels.

❖ Season some all-purpose flour with salt and chili powder, or cayenne and paprika, to taste, and add the cilantro. Toss the eggplant slices in the flour to coat evenly, then dip in the beaten egg. Let the excess egg to drain off.

❖ Heat a deep-fat fryer half-filled with oil to 350°F. Add the eggplant slices in batches so the pan is not crowded and fry until golden brown. Drain on paper towels. Serve hot with Sesame Dipping Sauce.

SESAME DIPPING SAUCE

Chojang 3

Sesame oil and toasted sesame seeds make a more richly flavored dipping sauce.

MAKES 6 TABLESPOONS

3 tablespoons soy sauce
1 teaspoon sesame oil
1½ tablespoons rice vinegar
1 teaspoon toasted sesame seeds
pinch of sugar
1 small scallion, finely chopped

❖ Combine the soy sauce, sesame oil and rice vinegar in a small bowl. Add the remaining ingredients and mix well.

STUFFED CUCUMBER PICKLE

Oisobagi

Use a potato peeler or the slicing disk of a food processor to slice the white radish. To serve, slice through the cucumbers completely and arrange on a plate.

FILLS ABOUT 3 1-PINT JARS

1½ pounds pickling cucumbers

salt

1-inch piece of fresh ginger, cut into paper thin slices

12 ounces white radish, very thinly sliced

2 tablespoons very finely chopped garlic

6 scallions, white and some green parts very thinly sliced

2½ teaspoons Korean chili powder, or cayenne pepper mixed with paprika

1½ teaspoons sugar

❖ Cut the cucumbers crossways, slightly diagonally, at ½-inch intervals but not going quite all the way through – the slices should remain attached at the bottom.

❖ Pour 4½ cups water into a bowl and stir in 4 tablespoons of salt until dissolved. Add the cucumbers and weight down with a plate to keep them submerged. Leave for 3–4 hours.

❖ Just before the cucumbers are ready, stack the ginger slices and cut into very thin strips.

Stack the white radish slices and cut across into very, very fine strips. If the strips are longer than 1 inch, cut them in half. Mix with the ginger, garlic, scallions, sugar, chili powder, or cayenne and paprika, and 2 teaspoons of salt.

❖ Lift the cucumbers from the liquid; reserve the liquid. Dry the cucumbers with paper towels. Fill the gaps between the cucumber slices with as much of the white radish stuffing as they will hold easily. Put into a bowl. Add any remaining white radish stuffing and liquid from it. Cover and leave for 8 hours.

❖ Carefully pack the cucumbers fairly tightly into clean, dry 1-pint jars. Push any loose stuffing between the cucumbers and pour in all the juices from the bowl. Push the cucumbers down; if the liquid does not cover them by ½ inch, add some of the reserved cucumber soaking water.

❖ Cover loosely and leave for 3–6 days until the pickle has soured to your taste. Seal tightly and keep until required. It will keep for up to a year.

SPICED TURNIP PICKLE

Sunmukimchi

Turnip is a very popular root vegetable in Korea, used in many everyday recipes as well as in pickles.

FILLS A 1 ½-CUP JAR

2 turnips, each weighing about 5 ounces, peeled, halved lengthways and thinly sliced

1 ½ teaspoons salt

3 garlic cloves, finely chopped

1 scallion, white and green part finely chopped

1 dried red chili, seeded and coarsely crushed

❖ Rub 1 teaspoon of the salt into the turnip slices, then put into a bowl. Leave for 3 hours, stirring the slices every 30 minutes.

❖ Drain the turnips and rinse under running cold water. Drain again, then mix with the remaining ingredients.

❖ Pack into a clean, dry jar, then cover with cold water. Put a saucer on the jar and leave for 6–8 days until the pickle turns sour.

❖ Cover the jar with a vinegar-proof lid and store in a cool, dry place for up to a year.

SPICED SWEET POTATO SLICES

Kogumajon

Traditionally, these potato slices are served with a dipping sauce but they can also be served as a vegetable accompaniment.

SERVES 4

2 sweet potatoes, cut diagonally into ¼-inch thick slices

salt

all-purpose flour for coating

chili powder

1 large egg, beaten

vegetable oil for frying

Vinegar Dipping Sauce (see page 32) to serve

❖ Add the sweet potato slices to a saucepan of boiling salted water and cook for about 5 minutes. Drain well and dry on paper towels.

❖ Season the flour with chili powder, then coat the sweet potato slices evenly in the seasoned flour. Dip in beaten egg.

❖ Heat a thin layer of vegetable oil in a wide skillet. Add a layer of sweet potato slices, and fry for about 4 minutes on each side.

❖ Transfer to paper towels to drain. Serve hot with Vinegar Dipping Sauce.

CABBAGE PICKLE

Kimchi I

This is a standard cabbage *kimchi*. Some of the cabbage can be replaced by thinly sliced white radish, if liked.

FILLS ABOUT 2 2-QUART JARS

2 pounds Chinese cabbage

salt

6 scallions, white and green parts thinly sliced

4 garlic cloves, crushed and finely chopped

2 tablespoons finely chopped fresh ginger

1 tablespoon Korean chili powder, or cayenne
    pepper mixed with paprika

1 teaspoon sugar

❖ Quarter the Chinese cabbage lengthways, then cut each quarter widthways into approximately 2-inch pieces.

❖ Pour 6¼ cups water into a large bowl and stir in 3 tablespoons salt until dissolved. Add the cabbage and weight down with a plate to keep the pieces submerged.

❖ Cover and leave for 12 hours, stirring the cabbage occasionally. Using a slotted spoon, remove the cabbage from the bowl, and reserve the salted water.

❖ Mix the cabbage with the remaining ingredients and 1 teaspoon salt. Pack into clean, dry 2-quart jars. Pour in enough of the reserved salted water to cover the cabbage; leave a space of 1 inch at the top of the jar. Cover the jar loosely with a non-metallic lid and leave for 3–6 days until the pickle has become sour enough for your taste. Cover tightly and keep in a cold, dark place. It will keep in these conditions for up to 1 year.

ABOVE *Many crafts and farming techniques
are still based largely on tradition.*

PICKLED GARLIC

Manul

Green garlic is used in Korea for this recipe, but it works very well with ordinary garlic if the heads are made up of large, plump cloves. After pickling, the cut garlic heads are cut crossways to make attractive slices.

FILLS A 1-CUP JAR

2 heads of garlic with plump cloves

½ cup rice vinegar

½ cup soy sauce

2 tablespoons sugar

1 teaspoon salt

❖ Put the garlic in a clean, dry 1-cup jar. Bring the remaining ingredients to a boil in a small saucepan, then simmer gently until reduced by half. Pour over the garlic. Cover tightly and leave for 2 months. It will keep for up to a year in a cool, dry place.

INSTANT CUCUMBER PICKLE

Khachori

This is a very convenient version of *kimchi* as it can be eaten as soon as it has been chilled.

SERVES 6-8

1 pound cucumbers

2¼ teaspoons salt

1 garlic clove, crushed and finely chopped

3½-inch piece of white radish, cut into fine strips

2 scallions, white and green parts thinly sliced

1-inch piece of fresh ginger, crushed to a pulp

1½ teaspoons Korean chili powder, or cayenne
   pepper mixed with paprika

2 teaspoons Crushed Toasted Sesame Seeds
   (see page 22)

1 tablespoon sesame oil

❖ Cut the cucumber into 2-inch lengths, then cut each piece lengthways in half. Place each half skin-side up and slice across. Put the slices in a colander, and toss with 2 teaspoons of the salt. Leave for 3 hours.

❖ Drain the cucumber gently, squeezing out as much water as possible.

❖ Mix the cucumber with the remaining salt, garlic, white radish, scallions, ginger and chili powder, or cayenne and paprika. Cover and chill. Drain off the liquid from the vegetables, then toss them with the sesame seeds and sesame oil. This will keep for a day or two in the refrigerator.

(clockwise from top right) Pickled Garlic, Instant Cucumber Pickle and Stuffed Cabbage Pickle (p64) ▶

STUFFED CABBAGE PICKLE

Kimchi 2

Salted fish, especially anchovies, are a popular addition to *kimchis*; the fish dissolve during the fermentation and storage, enriching the flavor of the *kimchi*, not giving it a fishy taste. For convenience, I have used fish sauce instead of salted anchovies.

FILLS A 1-CUP JAR

6 tablespoons salt

½ Chinese cabbage, about 8 ounces

6-ounce piece of white radish, halved crossways

4 scallions, coarsely chopped

4 garlic cloves, crushed and finely chopped

1-inch piece of fresh ginger, crushed and finely chopped

1 tablespoon Korean chili powder, or cayenne pepper mixed with paprika

1 teaspoon sugar

2 tablespoons fish sauce

❖ Pour 4½ cups water into a large bowl and stir in all but ¼ teaspoon of the salt until dissolved. Add the cabbage and put a plate on top to keep it submerged. Leave for 8–10 hours.

❖ Cut the white radish into thin strips, then mix well with the remaining ingredients, including the remaining salt. Drain the cabbage well, then squeeze hard to remove as much water as possible.

❖ Place the cabbage cut-side up. Beginning with the outer leaves, pack the white radish mixture between each leaf.

❖ Fold the cabbage leaves and pack them into a clean, dry jar. Add any remaining white radish mixture. Cover loosely with vinegar-proof lids and leave for at least 3 days until sour enough for your taste. Push the cabbage down so it remains beneath the liquid that is produced. Cover tightly and keep in a cold place until required. It will keep for up to a year.

large tuna.

STIR-FRIED SQUID WITH CHILIES AND VEGETABLES

Ojhingubokum

Both the hot, fermented bean paste, *kochujang*, and Korea's excellent coarsely pounded red chili powder, are used in this spicy dish. The Korean chili powder adds a characteristic bright, carmine pink color. If necessary you can always use cayenne pepper mixed with paprika to obtain the same result. Chili bean paste can also be substituted for the *kochuchang*.

SERVES 3-4

1¼ pounds cleaned squid

3 tablespoons vegetable oil

1 onion, thinly sliced

2 garlic cloves, crushed

1 carrot, thinly sliced lengthways

1 zucchini, thinly sliced lengthways

2–3 long fresh red chilies, thinly sliced lengthways

2 long fresh green chilies, thinly sliced lengthways

1 tablespoon *kochujang* (see page 69) or chili bean paste

about ½ teaspoon Korean chili powder, or cayenne pepper mixed with paprika

1 teaspoon sugar

salt and freshly ground black pepper

2 scallions, white and green parts sliced diagonally

2 teaspoons sesame oil

toasted sesame seeds to garnish

❖ Cut open each squid body so that it lies flat, then cut across into 2½- by ½-inch pieces. Cut the tentacles into 2½-inch lengths.

❖ Bring a large saucepan of water to a boil. Add all the squid simultaneously and remove from the heat. Stir immediately and continue to stir until the squid turns white, about 40 seconds. Drain well and discard the water.

❖ Heat the oil in a large skillet over a moderate heat. Add the onion, garlic and carrot. Stir for 30–40 seconds, then add the zucchini, chilies and 2 teaspoons *kochujang* or chili bean paste, half the chili powder or cayenne and paprika. Stir for 30 seconds. Stir in the squid, remaining *kochujang* and chili powder or cayenne and paprika, sugar and salt and pepper. Cook slowly for 2 minutes, then add the scallions and sesame oil. Tip into a warm serving dish and garnish with toasted sesame seeds.

OYSTERS

Kulhoe

Instead of the traditional lemon juice, try spooning a little of this Korean sauce over oysters before sucking them, with their juices, from their shells.

SERVES 4

12–24 oysters in the shell, opened

SAUCE

2 tablespoons rice vinegar

I tablespoon *kochujang* (see below) or chili bean paste

½-inch piece of fresh ginger, crushed and finely chopped

I ½ teaspoons sugar

few drops of soy sauce to taste

❖ Mix together all the ingredients for the sauce, adjusting the levels of flavorings to taste. Pour into a small bowl. Cover and chill until ready to serve.

❖ Before serving, spoon the prepared sauce over the oysters.

HOMEMADE RED PEPPER PASTE

Kochujang

Kochujang is an important seasoning and flavoring (see page 11). It used to be made at home, from home-fermented soybeans, but even in Korea it is often bought ready-made nowadays. In the West it can only be purchased from Korean stores, but an approximation can be made at home quite easily using fairly readily available ingredients.

MAKES ABOUT 7 TABLESPOONS

4 tablespoons brown or red miso

I ½ tablespoons paprika

I teaspoon cayenne pepper

I tablespoon sugar

❖ Mix all the ingredients together in a small bowl. Keep in a screw-top jar in a cool, dark place, It will keep for up to six months in these conditions.

◀ *Oysters*

BROILED SCALLOP KEBABS

Paejusanjok

Rice vinegar begins to "cook" the scallops in the same way that lime juice "cooks" fish when making Mexican *ceviche*, so the scallops need only brief cooking under the broiler if they are not to become overcooked.

SERVES 2-4

12 large scallops
1 garlic clove, crushed and finely chopped
1 tablespoon scallion, green part, finely chopped
2 tablespoons soy sauce
2 teaspoons rice vinegar
1 tablespoon sesame oil
½-inch piece of fresh ginger, grated
2 teaspoons Crushed Toasted Sesame Seeds
   (see page 22)
pinch of chili powder

❖ Cut each scallop in half horizontally. Thread the scallops onto skewers and lay them in a shallow, non-metallic dish.

❖ Mix together the remaining ingredients and pour over the scallops. Turn the skewers over and leave for 15–30 minutes, turning occasionally.

❖ Preheat the broiler.

❖ Lift the skewers from the marinade and cook under the broiler for about 4 minutes, turning occasionally and brushing with the marinade.

STEAMED CRAB

Ke-tchim

The crab mixture can be steamed in a large crab shell. It is well worth
using fresh crab meat for better flavor and texture.

SERVES 6

2 ounces bean sprouts

scant ¼ cup medium-firm bean curd

about 2 cups finely chopped, mixed white and
    brown crab meat

½-inch piece of fresh ginger, grated

2 scallions, very finely chopped

1 teaspoon sesame oil

salt and freshly ground black pepper

1 tablespoon all-purpose flour

1 egg, beaten

diagonally sliced white and green parts
    of scallion for garnish

❖ Add the bean sprouts to a saucepan of
boiling water. Quickly return to a boil and boil
for 1 minute. Tip into a colander and rinse
under cold water. Drain well, then squeeze out
as much water as possible. Chop finely.

❖ Wrap the bean curd in a clean cloth and
squeeze firmly to express surplus liquid. Finely
crumble the bean curd. Mix the crab meat, bean
sprouts, bean curd, ginger, scallions, sesame oil
and seasonings together. Divide between six
individual heatproof dishes.

❖ Sift the flour over the tops of the dishes,
then brush with beaten egg. Put in a steaming
basket. Cover the dishes with baking
parchment and cover the steaming basket. Put
the steaming basket over a saucepan of boiling
water and steam the crab for about 10 minutes.
Garnish with scallions.

BROILED FISH

Saengsongui

For this dish you can use red snapper, sea bass, pompano, grey mullet or trout. If preferred, fish steaks or cutlets can be used in place of a whole fish; it is not necessary to slash these, and they will only need to be cooked for 3–5 minutes on each side, depending on thickness and type.

SERVES 2-4

1½-pound whole fish, scaled and
   cleaned
1½ tablespoons rice vinegar
2 tablespoons sesame oil
3 tablespoons soy sauce
2 garlic cloves, crushed and finely
   chopped
1-inch piece of fresh ginger, grated
1 scallion, white and green part finely
   sliced
1½ tablespoons Crushed Toasted
   Sesame Seeds (see page 22)
2 teaspoons Korean chili powder, or
   cayenne pepper mixed with paprika
2 teaspoons sugar
freshly ground black pepper

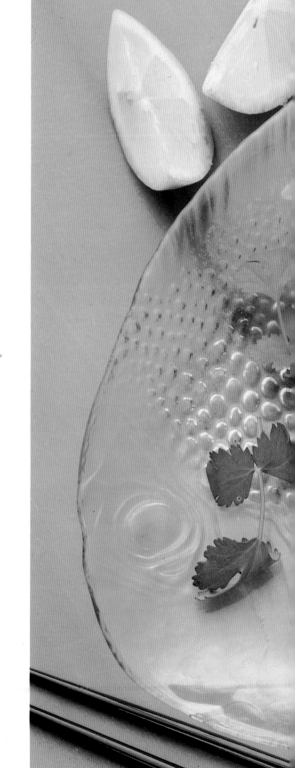

❖ With the point of a sharp knife, cut four deep diagonal slashes on each side of the fish.

❖ Mix together the remaining ingredients and rub one-third into the fish, taking care to work it deep into the slashes.

❖ Preheat the broiler. Broil the fish about 6 inches away from the heat for 6–7 minutes a side, basting occasionally with another third of the sauce.

❖ Transfer the fish to a warm serving plate and pour over the remaining sauce.

FRIED FISH STRIPS

Saengsonjon

These are cut into strips similar to French *goujons*, but they are lighter to
eat as they are coated in just egg and flour rather than batter, and shallow-
rather than deep-fried.

SERVES 3-4

1 ¼ pounds white fish fillets such as cod or
　flounder
1 plump garlic clove, halved lengthways
seasoned all-purpose flour for coating
1–2 eggs, beaten
oil for frying
Seasoned Dipping Sauce (see page 75) to serve

❖ Rub the fish with the cut side of the garlic
halves, then thinly slice the fish diagonally.

❖ Coat the fish in seasoned flour, then dip in
beaten egg and let the excess egg drain off.

❖ Heat a shallow layer of oil in a skillet. Add
the fish strips, in batches if necessary so they are
not crowded, and fry for about 5 minutes,
depending on thickness. Transfer to paper
towels to drain, then serve hot with Seasoned
Dipping Sauce.

SEASONED DIPPING SAUCE

Yangyumjang

This version of *chojang* has the most complex flavors.

MAKES 7 TABLESPOONS

4 tablespoons soy sauce

2 teaspoons sesame oil

I tablespoon rice vinegar

about ¼–½ fresh red or green chili

2 teaspoons toasted sesame seeds

pinch of sugar

½–I small garlic clove, finely chopped

❖ Combine the soy sauce, sesame oil and rice vinegar in a small bowl. Deseed the chili and chop finely. Add to the bowl with remaining ingredients and mix well.

KOREAN FISH STEW

Maeuctana

Like other great fish stew-soups of the world, such as *bouillabaisse*, this is made with a mixture of fish and shellfish that happen to be available.

SERVES 4

4 dried Chinese black mushrooms, soaked in
    ⅔ cup hot water for 30 minutes

5 cups Korean Chicken Stock (see page 16)

I½–I¾ pounds whole fish, cut into large chunks
    or filleted and cut into 2-inch pieces

about I tablespoon *kochujang* (see page 69) or
    chili bean paste

2 teaspoons sesame oil

salt and freshly ground black pepper

4 scallions, finely chopped

I red bell pepper, chopped

12 fresh clams, cleaned

4 ounces young fresh spinach leaves

diagonally sliced scallion leaves and sesame oil to
    garnish

❖ Drain the mushrooms, reserving the liquid. Cut away and discard the mushroom stalks, and slice the caps. Strain the reserved liquid into a saucepan. Add the fish pieces and the stock. Bring to a boil. Skim off any scum, then simmer for 30 minutes. Strain the stock and return it to the saucepan. Add *kochujang* to taste. Lightly season the fish and sprinkle with the sesame oil. Leave for 30 minutes.

❖ Add the scallions and red bell pepper to the stock. Bring to a boil and add the clams. Cook for about 2 minutes, then add all the fish and spinach. Bring just to a simmer, then cook slowly for about 3 minutes, until the fish is opaque; discard any clams that remain closed. Garnish and serve.

SHRIMP IN JACKETS

Saeutigim

When raw, tiger shrimp are dark grayish-brown with darker rings, but the shells turn rosy pink and the flesh pale pinkish white when cooked. They are quite expensive, but they are large and meaty – they can range from 3 inches up to enormous specimens of 10 inches – so three tiger shrimp of about 3–4 inches are enough for one portion.

SERVES 4

¾ cup all-purpose flour
2 teaspoons black sesame seeds
salt and freshly ground black pepper
1 egg, beaten
1–2 teaspoons sesame oil
12 raw tiger shrimp in their shells, about 3 inches long
vegetable oil for deep-frying
Vinegar Dipping Sauce (see page 32) to serve

❖ Stir together the flour, sesame seeds and seasoning. Stir in the egg and sesame oil, then add enough water (about ½ cup) to make a light coating batter. Set aside.

❖ Remove the heads and fine legs from the shrimp, leaving the tails intact. With a fine knife-point, slit along the back of each shrimp and remove the dark thread.

❖ Half fill a deep-fat fryer with vegetable oil and heat to 350°F.

❖ Stir the batter, then dip the shrimp into it. Let the excess batter drain off the shrimp, then deep-fry in batches for about 3–4 minutes until crisp and brown. Transfer to paper towels to drain. Keep warm while frying the remaining shrimp. Serve hot with Vinegar Dipping Sauce.

Beef is the favorite meat in Korea, a taste that is said to date back to the days of the Mongol invasion. Beef from cattle reared in the southern island of Cheju is particularly prized. Pork is less frequently eaten but it is now becoming more popular.

Chicken has for a long time been a mainstay of the Korean diet and there are many ways of cooking it.

QUICK BEEF

Pangjagui

The original concept of this recipe is that it is prepared and cooked quickly for people who are waiting to eat, but the beef can be marinated in a cool place with the remaining ingredients for 1–3 hours to give it extra flavor.

SERVES 2

8 ounces round steak

2 garlic cloves, crushed and finely chopped

2 scallions, finely chopped

2 tablespoons sesame oil

I tablespoon beef stock

salt and freshly ground black pepper

❖ Preheat the broiler. Cut the beef across the grain into slices about ½ inch thick. Score the slices on both sides. Put into a bowl.

❖ Mix the remaining ingredients together, and pour over the beef. Stir to coat in the marinade, then broil for 5–7 minutes, turning halfway through, until cooked to your liking.

PIQUANT LIVER

Kangui

This Korean treatment of liver makes it succulent, moist and tasty.

SERVES 2-4

8 ounces lambs' liver, thinly sliced, then cut into
  4- by I-inch pieces

2 tablespoons soy sauce

I garlic clove, cut into fine slivers

I tablespoon sesame seeds

I teaspoon sesame oil

about I tablespoon sugar

freshly ground black pepper

I large onion

I scallion, sliced and 8 snow peas for garnish

❖ Put the liver into a saucepan with the soy sauce, garlic, sesame seeds, sesame oil, sugar to taste and plenty of black pepper.

❖ Cut the onion into quarters, then slice each quarter crossways into four slices. Add to the pan and cook over a medium heat, lightly stirring occasionally, for 5 minutes.

❖ Add ⅔ cup water to the pan and simmer very slowly for about 5–8 minutes until the liver is tender.

❖ Garnish with scallion and snow peas.

◀ *Piquant Liver*

BEEF AND VEGETABLE HOTPOT

Chongol

Chongol is a communal one-pot meal, every person dipping into the pot to select their chosen morsels. Any number of a wide variety of ingredients can be added, according to what is available, or to suit the occasion. Traditionally, it is prepared over a burner at the table.

SERVES 4-6

1¼ pounds sirloin or filet mignon, partly frozen

3 cups brown veal or chicken stock

6 celery stalks, cut into 2-inch pieces

2 young carrots, finely sliced diagonally

8 crimini mushrooms

8 scallions, cut diagonally into 2-inch pieces

6 Chinese leaves, cut into 2-inch pieces

1½ 4-ounce cakes of bean curd, cut into 1-inch cubes

MARINADE

2 teaspoons sesame seeds

3 tablespoons sugar

1 fresh red chili, seeded and finely chopped

6 tablespoons soy sauce

1 plump garlic clove, finely crushed

◆ For the marinade, heat a dry heavy-bottomed saucepan, add the sesame seeds and toast until pale brown. Remove and crush finely. Mix with the remaining marinade ingredients.

◆ Slice the beef and cut into 1- by 2-inch strips. Put into a bowl. Pour over the marinade and stir to coat. Leave for 1 hour.

◆ Heat a dry heavy-bottomed pan. Remove the beef from the marinade and add to the pan. Cook briefly and quickly to sear the meat. Remove. Add the stock and any remaining marinade to the pan and bring to a boil. If using a fondue pot, boil the stock in a saucepan, then pour into the fondue pot.

◆ Add the celery and carrots to the pot. Boil for 5 minutes, then add the mushrooms, scallions, Chinese leaves, bean curd and beef. Simmer together for 2–3 minutes, then lower the heat so the stock simmers slowly while the chongol is eaten.

BRAISED BEEF WITH CARROTS AND ONIONS

Kalbitchim I

The beef is marinated, then cooked slowly for a long time so that
it can easily be removed from the bone with chopsticks.

SERVES 4

3 pounds beef short ribs

1½ tablespoons vegetable oil

2 carrots, cut into chunks

1 onion, cut into chunks

sesame seeds, cilantro and pine nuts for garnish

MARINADE

2 tablespoons sesame oil

6 tablespoons soy sauce

4 scallions, white and green parts thinly sliced

4 tablespoons rice wine or dry sherry

2 tablespoons Crushed Toasted Sesame Seeds
  (see page 22)

1-inch piece of fresh ginger, finely chopped

3 garlic cloves, crushed and finely chopped

freshly ground black pepper

❖ Separate the beef into individual ribs and
cut each one into 2-inch lengths. Make four
deep slashes in a lattice pattern on the meaty
sides of each piece of rib, going right through to
the bone. Put into a bowl. Add the marinade
ingredients, and stir together well. Cover and
leave in a cool place for 4 hours, stirring the
beef occasionally.

❖ Remove the beef from the marinade; reserve
the marinade.

❖ Heat the vegetable oil in a heavy flameproof
casserole and fry the beef for 5 minutes. Add the
onion and carrot chunks, and fry for 3 minutes
more. Pour in the reserved marinade and add
enough water just to cover the beef and
vegetables. Bring to a boil, cover and simmer
slowly for 1½–2 hours, turning the beef and
vegetables occasionally, until the beef is very
tender. Uncover the casserole about half to
three-quarters of the way through the cooking
so the sauce reduces.

❖ At the end of the cooking, boil the sauce
hard to reduce it to a thickish syrup, turning the
ribs to make sure they are evenly coated. Skim
any fat from the surface and serve garnished
with pine nuts, sesame seeds and cilantro.

BRAISED BEEF WITH WHITE RADISH

Kalbitchim 2

By the end of the cooking the pieces or rib and radish are coated in a thick, rich sauce.

SERVES 4

3 pounds beef short ribs
1 pound white radish, cut into 2-inch cubes
2 cups water
8 dried Chinese black mushrooms
4–6 garlic cloves, crushed
5 tablespoons soy sauce
1 tablespoon sesame oil
2 tablespoons Crushed Toasted Sesame Seeds
   (see page 22)
2 tablespoons light brown sugar
freshly ground black pepper

❖ Separate the beef into individual ribs and cut each one into 2-inch lengths. Make four deep slashes in a lattice pattern on the meaty sides of each piece of rib, going right through to the bone. Add to a large saucepan of boiling water. Bring the water to a boil again, and boil for 1 minute. Drain the beef and rinse under running cold water.

❖ Put the beef and white radish in a large skillet. Add the water and bring to a boil. Cover and simmer gently for 40 minutes.

❖ Meanwhile, soak the Chinese mushrooms in hot water for about 20 minutes. Lift the mushrooms from the water with a slotted spoon, and cut off and discard any hard parts and the hard stems.

❖ Add the garlic, soy sauce, sesame oil, sesame seeds, sugar and plenty of pepper to the beef. Raise the heat and bring to a boil again. Lower the heat to medium low and cook for 20 minutes with the lid slightly off.

❖ Turn the beef and radish over in the sauce. Add the mushrooms and continue to cook, partially covered, for 30 minutes more, basting occasionally, or until the beef is tender.

❖ Remove the lid, raise the heat and cook until the sauce is reduced to a few spoonfuls.

STIR-FRIED BEEF WITH GARLIC AND CHILIES

Soegogochubokkum

Garlic and chilies give the character to this simple, tasty stir-fry, but the number of each can be adjusted according to personal taste.

SERVES 3-4

1 pound sirloin steak, cut into strips

2 tablespoons soy sauce

1 scallion, white and green part thinly sliced

1½ teaspoons sesame oil

2 tablespoons rice wine or dry sherry

1½ teaspoons sugar

1½ tablespoons vegetable oil

3 garlic cloves, cut into slivers

4 fresh red chilies, seeded and cut into strips

½ egg, beaten, fried and cut into strips (see below) for garnish

toasted sesame seeds for garnish

❖ Put the beef in a bowl. Add the soy sauce, scallion, sesame oil, rice wine or dry sherry and sugar. Stir, then cool for 1 hour.

❖ Heat the oil in a skillet. Add the garlic and chilies, and stir-fry over a high heat until fragrant, about 1 minute. Remove with a slotted spoon and reserve.

❖ Lift the beef from the marinade, and add to the pan. Stir-fry for 2–3 minutes. Return the chilies and garlic to the pan. Add the marinade and cook, stirring, over a medium heat for about 2 minutes. Serve garnished with egg strips and toasted sesame seeds.

FRIED EGG STRIP GARNISH

Chon

A common garnish for Korean savory dishes. Lightly beaten eggs are fried one at a time to keep the mixture thin. Sometimes, the eggs are separated and the yolks and whites cooked separately.

SERVES 1

1 egg, lightly beaten

vegetable oil for frying

❖ Heat a very thin film of vegetable oil in a large skillet, preferably nonstick. Pour in the egg, and tilt and swirl the pan to spread the egg out in a thin even layer. Fry for 1–2 minutes until set underneath, then turn the "omelet" over and fry until set. Transfer the "omelet" to a wooden board, or a work surface, and roll it up. Cut into ¼-inch strips.

QUICK-COOK BEEF, BEAN CURD AND VEGETABLE "STEW"

Twoenjangchigae

Richness and depth is given to the flavor of this "stew" by making the stock with *twoenjang*, Korean fermented bean curd. The beef is then cooked for just 2 minutes.

SERVES 3-4

8 ounces sirloin or round
    steak, cut into 1- by 2-inch
    slices
2 teaspoons sesame oil
1½ teaspoons sugar
freshly ground black pepper
8 dried Chinese black
    mushrooms, soaked in hot
    water for 30 minutes,
    drained, and stalks removed
1 onion, thinly sliced into rings
1 zucchini, sliced
2 scallions, white and green
    parts sliced

1–2 fresh red chilies, seeded
    and thickly sliced
2 x 4-ounce cakes of medium-
    firm bean curd, cut into
    1½-inch chunks

STOCK

8 tablespoons *twoenjang*
    (fermented bean curd) or
    miso
2 garlic cloves, lightly crushed
1 onion, cut into chunks
1 carrot, cut into chunks
3 scallions, white and green
    parts cut into 3-inch lengths

❖ Put the *twoenjang* or miso in a strainer placed over a saucepan. Slowly pour through 4 cups of water, pushing the *twoenjang* or miso with the back of a wooden spoon so it is all pushed through. Add the remaining stock ingredients and bring to a boil. Cover and simmer slowly for 30 minutes.

❖ Meanwhile, mix the beef with the sesame oil, sugar and plenty of black pepper. Leave for 30 minutes.

❖ Drain the stock, squeezing out as much liquid as possible. Pour the stock back into the pan and add the mushroom caps, onion, zucchini, scallions and chilies. Bring to a boil, then simmer for 2 minutes. Add the beef slices to the stock with the bean curd. Return to a boil, then simmer for 2 minutes.

BEEF AND BEAN CURD PATTIES

Gogijon

These light patties are served as simple everyday fare in most Korean homes. The patties are usually small so that they can be lifted with the slim Korean chopsticks.

SERVES 4-6

8 ounces medium-firm bean curd

3 cups freshly ground lean beef

2 garlic cloves, crushed and finely chopped

2 scallions, white and green parts very finely chopped

1 tablespoon sesame oil

2 teaspoons soy sauce

4 teaspoons Crushed Toasted Sesame Seeds (see page 22)

all-purpose flour for coating

2 eggs, beaten

vegetable oil for frying

rice sticks and *kimchi* to serve

❖ Put the bean curd in a piece of cheesecloth or fine cloth and squeeze out as much water as possible. Press the bean curd through a strainer, then mix with the beef, garlic, scallions, sesame oil, soy sauce and sesame seeds. Form into patties about 1½ inches in diameter and just under ½ inch thick.

❖ Toss the patties in all-purpose flour to coat evenly, then dip in beaten egg.

❖ Heat a thin layer of vegetable oil in a large skillet. Add some of the patties to make a single layer and fry slowly for 2½–3 minutes on each side or until golden. Using a slotted spoon, transfer the patties to paper towels to drain while frying the remaining patties.

KOREAN MEATBALLS

Sogoki-chun

These flavorful meatballs are served as one of the side dishes in
a Korean meal. They are also good cold so a useful item for a picnic.

SERVES 2-3

2 cups lean ground beef

3 tablespoons soy sauce

2 scallions, finely chopped

2 garlic cloves, finely chopped

1 tablespoon Crushed Toasted Sesame Seeds
  (see page 22)

1½ teaspoons sesame oil

freshly ground black pepper

seasoned all-purpose flour for coating

2 eggs, lightly beaten

vegetable oil for frying

Vinegar Dipping Sauce (see page 32) to serve

❖ Mix together the beef, soy sauce, scallions,
garlic, sesame seeds, sesame oil and plenty of
pepper. Leave for 30 minutes.

❖ Form the meat mixture into flattened
rounds about 1½ inches in diameter. Toss in
seasoned flour to coat evenly, then dip in beaten
egg, letting excess egg drain off.

❖ Heat a little oil in a skillet, preferably
nonstick, and fry the meatballs until brown and
crisp on both sides and cooked through.

❖ Serve with Vinegar Dipping Sauce.

BROILED STEAK WITH SESAME

Tungshimgui

This is a very quick, simple treatment for well-flavored sirloin steak.
Use good quality meat and preferably meat that has not been frozen.

SERVES 3-4

1 or 2 pieces of sirloin steak, total weight
    about 1½ pounds, well chilled
1 garlic clove, crushed
2 tablespoons sesame oil
1 tablespoon toasted sesame seeds
salt

❖ Using a large, sharp knife, thinly slice the sirloin diagonally across the grain. Rub each slice with garlic and brush with sesame oil.

❖ Preheat the broiler or barbecue. Broil or grill the beef for 1–2 minutes on each side. Sprinkle with sesame seeds and salt and serve.

KOREAN "HOT MEAT"

Changjorim

The beef is served cold with its own spicy jelly as a side dish, and is eaten in small amounts. Because the jelly is an integral part of the dish, it is important to use a gelatinous cut of beef, such as shank. Adjust the number of chilies to suit your taste for "hot" foods.

SERVES 4-6

2 pounds beef shank
3 tablespoons sesame oil
6 tablespoons Japanese soy sauce
about 8 fresh red or green chilies, halved
    and seeded
1 red bell pepper, seeded and quite thinly sliced

❖ Put the meat into a saucepan. Add enough water just to cover it and bring to a boil. Skim the scum from the surface, then add the remaining ingredients. Cover the pan and simmer very slowly for 2–3 hours until the meat is so tender it is beginning to fall apart. Keep an eye on the water level to make sure the pan does not become dry, but do not drown the meat. At the end of the cooking, it should be surrounded by a thick sauce.

❖ Remove from the heat and let the meat cool in the liquid. Break the meat apart with a fork and serve with the jelly, chilies and sliced red bell pepper.

BROILED BEEF

Pulgogi

Pulgogi is one of the most popular Korean dishes. Pulgogi is also the name of the domed-shape metal hotplate that is put on a table-top burner for cooking the beef. A broiler and broiler rack or a barbecue can be used instead.

SERVES 4

4 scallions, coarsely chopped

3 garlic cloves, crushed and finely chopped

1 tablespoon Crushed Toasted Sesame Seeds
  (see page 22)

3 tablespoons soy sauce

2 teaspoons rice wine or dry sherry

1 tablespoon sesame oil

2 tablespoons sugar

freshly ground black pepper

1 ¼ pounds filet mignon, sirloin or round steak,
  frozen for 1 hour

vegetable oil for brushing

❖ Mix together the scallions, garlic, sesame seeds, soy sauce, rice wine or sherry, sesame oil, sugar, 2 tablespoons water and plenty of black pepper.

❖ Cut the beef crossways into ¼-inch thick slices. Lay in a shallow dish. Pour over the scallion mixture, cover and let marinate for 1 hour.

❖ Preheat the broiler or barbecue. Lightly oil a broiler rack or table-top grill plate. Cook the beef in batches in a single layer for about 1 minute on each side until browned on the outside but still pink inside.

ABOVE *Lush, green countryside is often the result of long, hot summers and plenty of rain.*

SPICED BARBECUED BEEF RIBS

Kalbigui

Beef, or pork, spareribs can be used instead of beef short ribs.
The traditional accompaniments are rice, a *kimchi* (see pages 40–64) and
a selection of salads.

SERVES 4

2 pounds beef short ribs, cut into 3-inch lengths

I tablespoon Crushed Toasted Sesame Seeds
  (see page 22)

4 tablespoons Japanese soy sauce

4 scallions, white parts only, sliced and crushed

3 garlic cloves, crushed and finely chopped

1½ tablespoons sesame oil

I-inch piece of fresh ginger, grated

2 teaspoons sugar

freshly ground black pepper

toasted sesame seeds for garnish

❖ Using a sharp knife, cut the meaty sides of the ribs through to the bone in a lattice pattern. This lets the marinade penetrate, tenderizes the meat and hastens the cooking. Put the ribs into a dish.

❖ Mix together the remaining ingredients, except the garnish, and pour over the meat. Stir to mix, then cover and leave for at least 3–4 hours, preferably overnight.

❖ Preheat the broiler or barbecue.

❖ Lift the beef from the marinade. Broil or grill the beef, brushing occasionally with the marinade, until it is a rich golden brown, 12–15 minutes on each side. Serve hot sprinkled with sesame seeds.

ABOVE *Ceremony plays a large part in Korean life; respect
for elders, religious events, and here, tea drinking.*

KOREAN BRAISED CHICKEN THIGHS

Takpokkum

Chicken thighs become richly flavored and very tender and succulent when steeped in a tasty marinade, then fried and braised in it.

SERVES 4

8 chicken thighs

4 scallions, white parts only, very finely chopped

1-inch piece of fresh ginger, grated

2 garlic cloves, crushed and chopped

4 tablespoons soy sauce

1 tablespoon sesame oil

1½ tablespoons Crushed Toasted Sesame Seeds
   (see page 22)

2 teaspoons sugar

vegetable oil for frying

1 red bell pepper, seeded and diced

2 scallions, white and pale green parts sliced
   diagonally

❖ Slash each chicken thigh three times and place in a shallow dish.

❖ Mix together the finely chopped scallions, ginger, garlic, soy sauce, sesame oil, sesame seeds and sugar. Pour over the chicken. Turn to coat with the sauce and leave in a cool place for about 4 hours, turning occasionally.

❖ Heat a little vegetable oil in a heavy flameproof casserole. Lift the chicken thighs from the marinade, add to the casserole and brown evenly. Pour in the marinade and enough water just to cover the chicken. Bring barely to simmering point. Cover the casserole and leave to cook gently for about 30–35 minutes, turning the chicken occasionally, until very tender.

❖ Add the red bell pepper and sliced scallions about 5 minutes before the end of cooking. If necessary, uncover the casserole toward the end of cooking to let the sauce reduce.

MARINATED THINLY SLICED CHICKEN BREAST

Takkooe

Traditionally, vegetables, rice and pickles are served with the chicken, but I also like to eat it with a crisp salad, or on firm white, crusty bread.

SERVES 3-4

3 tablespoons Japanese dark soy sauce

2 tablespoons sesame oil

1 tablespoon Crushed Toasted Sesame Seeds (see page 22)

1-inch piece fresh ginger, grated

2 garlic cloves, crushed

2 scallions, white and green parts thinly sliced into rings

2 tablespoons rice wine

salt and freshly ground black pepper

12 ounces skinned, boneless chicken breast, chilled

2 tablespoons vegetable oil

2 fresh hot red chilies, thickly sliced crossways

4 large brown mushrooms, oyster or shiitake, each cut into 4 slices

❖ Mix together the soy sauce, sesame oil and seeds, ginger, garlic, scallions, rice wine or sherry, salt and plenty of black pepper to taste.

❖ Holding the knife at a slight angle, cut across the chicken breasts to make ⅛-inch wide slices. Using a meat mallet or the flat side of a cleaver, pound each slice, at the same time dragging the mallet or cleaver across the slice. Lay the slices in a large, shallow dish, pouring some of the soy/sesame sauce over each layer. Cover and leave for 1 hour.

❖ Heat the vegetable oil in a large, preferably nonstick, skillet. Lift some of the chicken slices from the marinade and add to the pan so they lie flat in a single layer. Cook for 1 minute on each side until lightly browned and cooked through. Transfer to a warm plate and keep warm while frying the remaining chicken.

❖ When all the chicken has been cooked, add the chilies, mushrooms and remaining marinade to the pan. Stir and cook for 1 minute. Pour over the chicken and serve immediately.

STIR-FRIED CHICKEN

Tak

Prepare the vegetables while the chicken is marinating; then, when you start cooking, the dish is soon ready to serve.

SERVES 4

1 pound skinned, boneless chicken breasts,
  cut into strips
2 tablespoons soy sauce
1 tablespoon sugar
2 scallions, white and some green parts finely
  chopped
1-inch piece of fresh ginger, finely chopped
1½ teaspoons Crushed Toasted Sesame Seeds
  (see page 22)
freshly ground black pepper
1 small carrot, thinly sliced diagonally
3 dried Chinese black mushrooms, soaked for
  30 minutes in hot water
1½ tablespoons sesame oil
1 red bell pepper, seeded and cut into thin strips
Fried Egg Strip Garnish (see page 85)

❖ Put the chicken into a bowl.

❖ Mix together the soy sauce, sugar, scallions, ginger, sesame seeds and plenty of pepper. Pour over the chicken. Turn the chicken over and leave for 30 minutes. Remove from the marinade; reserve the marinade.

❖ Meanwhile, blanch the carrot in boiling water for 5 minutes. Drain and set aside.

❖ Drain the mushrooms, cut out and discard any hard patches and the stalks. Slice the mushroom caps.

❖ Heat the sesame oil in a skillet. Add the chicken and stir-fry for 2–3 minutes. Remove from pan and set aside. Add the mushrooms and carrots, and stir-fry for 2 minutes. Add the pepper and stir-fry for another minute.

❖ Return the chicken to the pan. Add the reserved marinade and bring to a boil. Stir and cook for 1 minute, then serve garnished with egg strips.

CHICKEN AND SCALLION KEBABS

Taksanjok

As good as these kebabs are when broiled, they are even better when cooked on a barbecue.

SERVES 4

about 1½ pounds skinned, boneless chicken
   thighs

1–2 bunches plump scallions, white parts only

4 tablespoons soy sauce

1 tablespoon sesame oil

2 teaspoons sugar

2 garlic cloves, crushed and finely chopped

¾-inch piece of fresh ginger, grated

1 tablespoon Crushed Toasted Sesame Seeds
   (see page 22)

diagonally sliced pale green parts of scallion for
   garnish

toasted sesame seeds for garnish

❖ Cut each chicken thigh into three lengths. Thread pieces of chicken and scallions alternately onto short skewers. Lay the skewers in a large, shallow dish.

❖ Mix together the remaining ingredients, except the garnishes, and pour over the skewers. Turn to coat with the sauce, then leave for 3–4 hours, turning occasionally.

❖ Preheat the broiler or barbecue.

❖ Lift the skewers from the marinade and broil or grill for about 10–15 minutes, turning occasionally and brushing with the remaining marinade. Serve garnished with scallions and toasted sesame seeds.

The traditional rhythm of the Korean year revolves around the ritual planting and harvesting of rice. Rice is the basic foodstuff of Koreans, and in per capita terms, their annual rice consumption is among the world's highest.

Rice is served, in small metal bowls, as the essential accompaniment to every meal; in hard times it is especially valuable for adding bulk to otherwise meager meals.

Noodles, which are regarded as a symbol of longevity, are also popular; noodle stalls are found on many town street corners. As well as noodles made from wheat flour, there are noodles made from buckwheat and mung bean flour.

Bean curd is an important food in the Korean diet. It is bought fresh every day from door-to-door salesmen, or made at home.

BOILED RICE

Ssalbap

Boiled rice not only provides a foundation for other dishes but is enjoyed on its own. For authentic results it is important to use the correct fat, short-grain variety – "Kokuho Rose" is a good brand to search for in ethnic stores. If you want to cook a different quantity of rice, simply follow the volume formula of rice to water – 1:1¼. Korean rice is never salted as the foods with which it is eaten are already sufficiently salty.

SERVES 4-6

scant 2 cups short-grain rice

❖ Put the rice in a large bowl and add water to cover it generously. Swish the rice around with your hand, at the same time rubbing the grains. When the water has become milky white, pour it away. Repeat the washing several times until the water is virtually clear. Leave the rice to soak for 2–3 hours. Tip the rice into a strainer, and leave to drain and dry for 1 hour.

❖ Put the rice into a heavy-bottomed saucepan. Add 2½ cups water and bring to a boil. Stir once, cover, and turn the heat right down. Cook the rice for 20 minutes, without removing the lid even once. Turn the heat up as high as it will go for 30 seconds, then turn it off, or remove the pan from the heat. Leave, without removing the lid at all, for 10–15 minutes before serving.

RICE WITH MILLET

Kijangbap

Traditionally, Kijangbap was prepared for the same reasons as Poribap (see page 103). A nuttier flavor can be obtained by toasting the millet, prior to boiling, in a dry saucepan over a moderate heat for 3 minutes.

SERVES 2-4

1½ cups short-grain rice, washed and soaked (see above)

⅔ cup millet

❖ Put the rice and millet into a saucepan. Add 3 cups water and bring to a boil. Stir once, cover, and turn the heat right down. Cook the rice for 20 minutes, without removing the lid even once. Turn the heat up as high as it will go for 30 seconds, then turn it off, or remove the pan from the heat. Leave, without removing the lid at all, for 10–15 minutes before serving.

RICE AND MUSHROOMS

Posotbap

Using mushrooms (of which Koreans are very fond) with a small amount
of beef to flavor rice is a good way of boosting the meaty flavor and giving
the illusion that there is more meat than there actually is.

SERVES 3-4

5 ounces lean ground beef

8 ounces open-cap mushrooms, preferably
   brown cap, chopped

2 garlic cloves, crushed and finely chopped

2 scallions, white and some green parts, chopped

2 tablespoons soy sauce

1½ teaspoons sesame oil

1 tablespoon Crushed Toasted Sesame Seeds
   (see page 22)

freshly ground black pepper

2 teaspoons vegetable oil

1 cup short-grain white rice, washed and soaked
   (see page 102)

very fine slices of red chili for garnish

❖ Mix together the beef, mushrooms, garlic,
scallions, soy sauce, sesame oil, sesame seeds
and plenty of pepper. Leave for at least 30
minutes.

❖ Heat the vegetable oil in a saucepan. Add the
mushroom and beef mixture, and stir until the
beef just changes color. Stir in the rice and 1¼
cups water. Cover and bring to a boil. Stir once
and cover again. Turn the heat to very low and
cook for 20–30 minutes, without removing the
lid even once. Turn the heat up as high as it will
go for 30 seconds, then turn it off, or remove
the pan from the heat. Leave, without removing
the lid at all, for 10–15 minutes. Stir before
serving garnished with very fine slices of red
chili.

RICE WITH BARLEY

Poribap

Barley used to be added to rice toward the end of summer when rice
stocks were getting low, to eke it out until the next crop was harvested.

SERVES 4

1½ cups short-grain rice, washed and soaked
   (see page 102)

⅔ cup pearl barley

❖ Put the rice and pearl barley into a
saucepan. Add 3 cups water and bring to a boil.
Stir once, cover, and turn the heat right down.
Cook the rice for about 20 minutes, without
removing the lid even once. Continue as in
recipe for Rice with Millet (see page 102).

RICE WITH SPINACH, BEAN SPROUTS AND LAVER

Pibimbap

This dish is generally eaten with a dipping sauce.

SERVES 4-6

8 ounces young fresh spinach, cut across into
   ¾-inch strips

8 ounces mung bean sprouts

1 garlic clove, chopped

1 carrot, cut into fine strips

2 scallions, white and green parts sliced diagonally

1½ sheets *kim* (*nori* or laver), cut into thin strips

2 teaspoons sesame oil

3 tablespoons soy sauce

2 teaspoons Crushed Toasted Sesame Seeds (see page 22)

½ teaspoon sugar

freshly ground black pepper

scant 2 cups short-grain rice, washed and soaked (see page 102)

❖ Add the spinach and bean sprouts to a large saucepan of water. Cover and quickly return to a boil. Boil for 1 minute, then tip into a colander. Drain well, then squeeze out as much water as possible. Mix with the remaining ingredients except the rice and leave for 30 minutes.

❖ Drain the rice and put into a saucepan with the vegetable mixture and 2½ cups water. Stir, then cover and bring to a boil. Stir once, cover again, and turn the heat to very low. Cook for 20–30 minutes, without removing the lid even once. Turn the heat up as high as it will go for 30 seconds, then turn it off, or remove the pan from the heat. Leave, without removing the lid at all, for 10–15 minutes before serving.

RICE, NOODLES AND BEAN CURD

COLD NOODLES WITH VEGETABLES

Kuksu

This is a vegetarian version of Kuksu, a popular noodle dish which is served surrounded by small bowls of condiments, relishes and side dishes, the most important of which are soy sauce, Korean chili powder, and *kimchis* (see pages 40–64). If you are unable to buy *son myon* noodles which are available from Korean food stores, use vermicelli and cook according to the directions on the package.

SERVES 4

3 tablespoons soy sauce

I tablespoon sugar

I tablespoon sesame oil

5 dried Chinese black mushrooms, soaked
   for 30 minutes in hot water

4 ounces bean sprouts

I pound young fresh spinach leaves, stalks
   removed

scant 2 cups vegetable stock

8 ounces *son myon* noodles or vermicelli

green part of I scallion, diagonally sliced

I tablespoon Crushed Toasted Sesame Seeds
   (see page 22)

very small pinch of Korean chili powder,
   or cayenne pepper mixed with paprika

❖ Mix together 2 tablespoons of the soy sauce, 2 teaspoons of the sugar and the sesame oil.

❖ Drain the mushrooms, and cut out and discard the stalks and any woody parts. Thinly slice the caps.

❖ Bring 3 cups water to a boil in a saucepan and add the remaining sugar. Put the bean sprouts into a strainer and lower the strainer into the water. Return the water to a boil and cook the bean sprouts for 20 seconds. Remove the strainer of bean sprouts from the water and rinse them under running cold water. Leave to drain completely.

❖ Add the spinach to the saucepan and boil for 2 minutes or until wilted. Drain, rinse under running cold water and drain again.

❖ Pour the stock into a saucepan. Add the remaining soy sauce and bring to a boil. Add the noodles and boil for about 3 minutes until just tender. Quickly remove the noodles from the water using a slotted spoon and put into a warm serving dish. Add the spinach and mushrooms to the liquid, and heat through, then quickly remove. Season with the soy sauce mixture and pile onto the noodles. Keep warm.

❖ Heat the bean sprouts in the stock, then remove and quickly season with the remaining soy sauce mixture. Place on top of the spinach and mushrooms. Pour the remaining stock around the noodles and sprinkle with the scallion, sesame seeds and a little chili powder or cayenne mixed with paprika.

CELLOPHANE NOODLES WITH VEGETABLES

Chapchae

Chapchae is a colorful vegetable-packed noodle dish with a multitude of different textures. After the vegetables have been prepared, it is very quick to assemble and cook.

SERVES 4

6 dried Chinese black mushrooms, soaked in
    hot water for 30 minutes

5 ounces young fresh spinach leaves

2 Chinese cabbage leaves

3 shiitake or oyster mushrooms, thinly sliced

4 scallions, white and green parts thickly sliced
    diagonally

1 small zucchini, cut into fine strips

1 carrot, cut into fine strips

4 tablespoons vegetable oil

1 tablespoon sesame oil

3 garlic cloves, crushed and finely chopped

2 small fresh red chilies, seeded and cut into
    fine strips

2 ounces cellophane noodles, soaked for
    30 minutes and drained

1 tablespoon soy sauce

1 teaspoon sugar

salt

❖ Drain the dried mushrooms, and cut out and discard the stems and any hard parts. Thinly slice the mushroom caps.

❖ Add the spinach to a large saucepan of boiling water. Cover and quickly return to a boil. Boil for 2 minutes, then drain and rinse under running cold water. Drain well and squeeze out as much water as possible. Separate the leaves.

❖ Cut away and discard the curly outer part of the Chinese cabbage leaves, saving only the "V" shaped core of the leaves. Cut this into fine strips, then mix with the spinach, dried and fresh mushrooms, scallions, zucchini and carrot until well mixed.

❖ Heat the vegetable oil and sesame oil in a deep skillet. Add the garlic and chili, and stir-fry for 10 seconds. Add the mixed vegetables and stir-fry for 3–4 minutes until the vegetables are tender but still crisp. Turn the heat to low and stir in the noodles, soy sauce, sugar and salt. Cook for 2 minutes, then serve.

RICE WITH BEEF AND BEAN SPROUTS

Kongamulbap

This is a dish eaten by poorer people as adding plain rice and bean sprouts to beef makes the meat go further.

SERVES 3-4

2 tablespoons soy sauce

2 garlic cloves, crushed and chopped

2 scallions, white and a little green part
   finely chopped

1½ tablespoons Crushed Toasted
   Sesame Seeds (see page 22)

1 tablespoon sesame oil

freshly ground black pepper

5 ounces lean beef, chilled

1 tablespoon vegetable oil

1 cup short-grain rice, washed, soaked
   and drained (see page 102)

8 ounces bean sprouts

very thin strips of red chili for garnish

❖ Mix the soy sauce, garlic, scallions, sesame seeds, sesame oil and pepper in a bowl.

❖ Slice the beef very thinly, stack the slices, and cut into strips. Stir into the bowl with the soy mixture to coat evenly and leave for 1 hour, stirring two or three times.

❖ Heat the vegetable oil in a large saucepan. Add the beef and stir-fry for 2–3 minutes until darker brown. Stir in the rice and bean sprouts, then add 1½ cups water. Bring to a boil. Stir once, cover, and turn the heat to very low. Cook the rice for 20 minutes, without removing the lid even once. Turn the heat up as high as it will go for 30 seconds, then turn it off, or remove the pan from the heat. Leave, without removing the lid at all, for 10–15 minutes. Serve garnished with very thin strips of red chili.

RICE, NOODLES AND BEAN CURD

RICE WITH SOYBEAN SPROUTS

Kongnamulbab

The bean sprouts provide a crisp contrast to the softness of the rice.

SERVES 4-6

8 ounces soybean sprouts.

scant 2 cups short-grain rice, washed and soaked
(see page 102)

❖ Add the bean sprouts to a saucepan of boiling water, cover and quickly return to a boil. Boil for 2 minutes, then drain.

❖ Drain the rice and put it into a saucepan. Put the bean sprouts on top and pour in 2½ cups water. Cover and bring to a boil. Stir once and cover again. Turn the heat to very low and cook for 20–30 minutes, without removing the lid. Turn the heat up high for 30 seconds, then turn it off. Leave for 10–15 minutes before serving.

BEANS WITH MIXED GRAINS

Ogokbap

The combination of red and black beans and three different grains make this a colorful dish with many different tastes and textures.

SERVES 4

⅓ cup red kidney beans, soaked overnight

⅓ cup black kidney beans, soaked overnight

1 cup short-grain rice, washed and soaked
(see page 102)

2 tablespoons millet

2 tablespoons pearl barley

◀ *Beans with Mixed Grains*

❖ Drain the beans, and add to a saucepan of boiling water. Cover and bring to a boil. Boil for 10 minutes, then simmer for 1–1½ hours until just tender; the time will depend on the beans. Drain them, reserving the water.

❖ Drain the rice. Put all the ingredients in a saucepan. Add 1¾ cups of the bean cooking water and bring to a boil. Stir once, then cover and turn the heat to very low. Cook for 20–30 minutes, without removing the lid even once. Turn the heat up as high as it will go for 30 seconds, then turn it off, or remove the pan from the heat. Leave, without removing the lid at all, for 10–15 minutes before serving.

FRESH BEAN CURD

Sundubu

Fresh bean curd, which is as white and soft as the white of poached eggs, is not difficult to make.

SERVES 4

2 cups yellow soybeans, soaked overnight
juice of 2 lemons

❖ Drain the beans and put half of them in a blender or food processor with 2½ cups warm water. Mix to a smooth purée. Pour the contents of the blender or food processor into a fine strainer lined with a large piece of cheesecloth and placed over a large bowl.

❖ Repeat with the remaining beans and another 2½ cups warm water, adding the purée to the strainer. Fold the cheesecloth over the pulp in the strainer and press firmly to extract as much liquid as possible.

❖ Return the residue in the strainer to the blender or food processor and add another 2½ cups warm water. Mix again for a couple of minutes, then pour into the strainer to drain. Discard the residue in the strainer. The thickish white liquid is soy milk.

❖ Bring the soy milk to a boil in a large saucepan. As soon as it begins to rise in the pan, lower the heat and simmer the milk, uncovered, for 15–20 minutes, stirring occasionally.

❖ Remove from the heat and stir in the lemon juice, which should make the milk curdle. Pour the curds and liquid into a fine strainer lined with a large clean piece of cheesecloth, and leave to drain.

❖ To make medium-firm bean curd, fold the cheesecloth over the curds, cover the surface of the curd with a weight (a heavy saucepan will do) and let drain for 15 minutes. To make firm bean curd, let drain for 2 hours. It will keep for up to two days.

ABOVE *The autumn harvest is a very important time of year, since winters tend to be long and often harsh.*

BRAISED BEAN CURD WITH PORK

Tubujorim I

This is another family way of braising bean curd.

SERVES 4

2 tablespoons soy sauce

1 teaspoon sesame seeds

2 tablespoons sugar

1½ tablespoons *kochujang* **(see page 69) or chili bean paste**

2 garlic cloves, crushed and finely chopped

1-inch piece of fresh ginger, grated

1½ teaspoons Crushed Toasted Sesame Seeds (see page 22)

12 ounces lean pork loin, very thinly sliced on the diagonal

3 tablespoons vegetable oil

2 4-ounce cakes of medium-firm bean curd

scallions, shredded diagonally for garnish

❖ Mix together the soy sauce, sesame seeds, sugar, *kochujang*, garlic and ginger.

❖ Lay the pork slices in a shallow dish and pour over the soy sauce mixture. Coat the pork with the mixture and leave for 30 minutes.

❖ Heat half the vegetable oil in a skillet. Add the pork mixture and cook for 12–15 minutes, turning the pork halfway through, until cooked through. Add a little water, as necessary, to keep the mixture fairly liquid.

❖ Meanwhile, cut each bean curd cake horizontally in half, then cut across each half into three pieces. Fry in the remaining oil in another skillet for about 3 minutes on each side, until golden. Transfer to paper towels.

❖ Pour the oil from the second skillet, then make a layer of bean curd in the pan. Cover with some of the pork mixture. Repeat, then cover and heat through gently for 5 minutes. Serve garnished with scallions.

POACHED BEAN CURD

Tofu

This plainly cooked bean curd can be eaten as it comes, or served with a dipping sauce. The role of cooking liquid in the serving dish is to keep the bean curd hot; it is not drunk. If preferred, the bean curd can be served in individual dishes with seaweed and bonito flakes.

SERVES 4

½ ounce wakame

3 cakes of medium-firm bean curd, each about 4 ounces

Vinegar Dipping Sauce (see page 32) to serve (optional)

❖ Bring 5½ pints water to a boil in a wide saucepan. Add the wakame and bean curd, and simmer gently for 5 minutes.

❖ Using a slotted spoon, transfer the bean curd to a warm serving dish deep enough to let the cakes be almost covered by the cooking liquid. Pour in simmering cooking liquid to come three-quarters of the way up the sides of the bean curd cakes. Serve straightaway, accompanied by vinegar dipping sauce, if liked.

FRIED BEAN CURD

Tububuchim

A little sesame oil adds a subtle yet distinctive flavor that "lifts" simple fried bean curd.

SERVES 6

4 x 4-ounce cakes of medium-firm bean curd
vegetable and sesame oil for frying
Vinegar Dipping Sauce (see page 32) to serve

❖ Cut the bean curd into rectangles approximately 1½ by ¾ by ¾ inches. Dry on paper towels.

❖ Heat a thin film of vegetable oil mixed with a little sesame oil in a nonstick skillet over a medium heat. Add half the bean curd and cook for 3 minutes on each side until golden. Using a slotted spoon, transfer to paper towels to drain while frying the remaining bean curd in the same way.

❖ Serve the bean curd on a warm plate with Vinegar Dipping Sauce.

BRAISED BEAN CURD WITH SESAME SEEDS

Tubujorim 2

Braised bean curd is a typical dish of Korean home cooking. Serve braised bean curd as a side dish, accompanied by rice and vegetables, and meat or fish as liked.

SERVES 2-4

2 tablespoons Japanese soy sauce

1 teaspoon sesame oil

1½ garlic cloves, crushed and chopped

2 teaspoons sugar

¼ teaspoon chili powder

2 teaspoons Crushed Toasted Sesame Seeds
   (see page 22)

2 scallions, white and green parts thinly sliced

7 ounces medium-firm bean curd, cut into
   ¼-inch thick rectangular slices

1½ tablespoons vegetable oil

freshly ground black pepper

◆ Mix together the soy sauce, sesame oil, garlic, sugar, chili powder, sesame seeds and scallions. Set aside.

◆ Put the bean curd in a single layer between two layers of paper towels. Cover with a plate and put a weight on the plate. Leave for 30 minutes or so.

◆ Heat the vegetable oil in a large skillet. Add the bean curd in a single layer and fry for about 1½ minutes on each side until browned. Using a slotted spatula, transfer to a large plate. Pour or wipe the oil from the pan.

◆ Return the bean curd to the pan in a single layer. Pour over the soy sauce mixture, partially cover the pan, and simmer for 6–7 minutes, turning the bean curd halfway through. Most of the sauce should be absorbed into the bean curd during this time.

◆ Transfer the bean curd to a warm plate and pour over the remaining sauce.

SWEET DISHES AND DRINKS

As in other Far Eastern countries, meals in Korea do not finish with a dessert; fresh fruit, of which there is a wonderful, luscious selection – plump strawberries, plums, persimmons, apples – is the most common way of rounding off a meal. However, sweet cakes and other sweetmeats are served for special occasions, such as birthdays, weddings and New Year's. Although Korea is surrounded by mighty tea-drinking nations, its people rarely touch it. They do, however, drink copiously of their own

BARLEY TEA

Poricha

Poricha is ubiquitous throughout Korea. In winter it is served hot, in summer it is served cold, sweetened with honey or sugar. Poricha has a distinctive, smoky taste, and is quite free of caffeine. Roast barley is available from Korean and Japanese food shops.

MAKES 3¾ CUPS

2 tablespoons roast barley
3¾ cups water

❖ Put the roast barley and water into a saucepan and bring to a boil. Lower the heat and simmer the tea until it is as strong as you like it. Strain.

ROLLED SESAME SLICES

Kkaegangjong

These uncooked cookies are rolled up like a jelly roll, then cut across into slices; this is easiest to do if you use a hot sharp knife.

SERVES 4

⅓ cup white sesame seeds
⅓ cup black sesame seeds
about ⅓ cup light brown sugar
8 tablespoons light corn syrup

❖ Heat the white and black sesame seeds in separate dry heavy skillets until they just begin to pop.

❖ Gently heat the sugar in the corn syrup, stirring until the sugar has dissolved. Mix half with the white sesame seeds and half with the black sesame seeds.

❖ Spread each mixture out on a sheet of waxed paper. Put another sheet of waxed paper on each and roll out. Remove the top sheets of waxed paper and invert the black sesame seed mixture onto the white sesame seed mixture. Remove the waxed paper now on top. Roll up the sesame seed mixtures firmly, enclosing the black in the white and using the underneath sheet of paper to help you. Leave until cold, then cut into slices.

Rolled Sesame Slices ▶

COOKIE BOWS

Maejakkwa

These crisp cookies are very moreish, but if you can resist eating them all soon after they are made, they will keep in an airtight container for several days.

SERVES 4-6

1 cup all-purpose flour
1 ½ tablespoons superfine sugar
3 tablespoons rice wine or dry sherry
vegetable oil for deep-frying
about ⅓ cup clear honey
chopped pine nuts for coating

❖ Stir together the flour and sugar, and slowly pour in the rice wine or dry sherry to make a smooth dough; add a little water if necessary. Knead lightly on a floured surface, then roll out lightly to a thin rectangle. Cut into 2- by 1-inch pieces. Cut a lengthways slit about 1 inch long in the center of each piece. Pull one end of each piece through the slit so the piece resembles a small bow shape.

❖ Heat the oil in a deep-fat fryer to 330°F. Add the bows and fry for 4–5 minutes until rich golden brown. Remove and drain briefly on a pad of paper towels.

❖ Meanwhile, slowly heat the honey (dilute with a little water if the honey is too thick). Dip the bows in the honey to coat, then sprinkle with chopped pine nuts.

Cookie Bows and Ginger Tea (p125) ▶

GINGER TEA

Saenggangcha

In addition to being a digestive, Saenggangcha is meant to be good for coughs and colds.

MAKES 4½ CUPS

3 1-inch pieces of fresh ginger, coarsely chopped
strip of orange peel
4–5 teaspoons clear honey
ground cinnamon for sprinkling
pine nuts for decorating

❖ Put the ginger, orange peel and honey in a saucepan and add 4½ Cups water. Bring to a boil, then simmer slowly for 15–20 minutes.

❖ Strain the tea and sprinkle a little cinnamon on top. Serve hot or cold with a few pine nuts floating on the surface.

SPICED HONEY CAKES

Yakkwa

In Korea, there are special *yakkwa* molds for shaping these deep-fried cakes. To get the juice from fresh ginger, squeeze a piece of peeled fresh ginger in a taint-free garlic press.

SERVES 4

1 cup self-rising flour
1 teaspoon ground cinnamon
grated zest of ½ lemon
2 tablespoons rice wine or dry sherry
2 tablespoons clear honey
1 teaspoon fresh ginger juice
2 tablespoons sesame oil
vegetable oil for deep-frying
sesame seeds for coating

❖ Sift the flour and cinnamon into a bowl. Stir in the lemon zest, then add the rice wine or sherry, honey, ginger juice and sesame oil and enough water to make a smooth dough. Knead the dough, then roll out on a lightly floured surface to about ¼ inch. Using a 1½-inch cookie cutter, cut into rounds.

❖ Heat the vegetable oil in a deep-fat fryer. Add the cakes in batches so they are not crowded, and fry until they rise to the surface and are light golden brown, about 3–5 minutes. Transfer to paper towels to drain. Sprinkle with sesame seeds.

◄ *Spiced Honey Cakes*

GINSENG TEA

Insamcha

Korean ginseng is believed to be the best, and in Korea (and elsewhere) ginseng is purported to cure all manner of ills, from insomnia to impotence. A favorite way of taking ginseng is in the form of a tea.

MAKES 3¾ PINTS

3 slices of red ginseng
½-inch piece of fresh ginger, sliced
3 jujubes (Chinese dates), cut into pieces

❖ Put all the ingredients into a saucepan. Add 3¾ cups water and bring to a boil. Lower the heat, cover and simmer for 1 hour.

❖ Strain into cups. Add pieces of jujube, gingseng and ginger to each cup if liked.

RICE TEA

Sungnyung

When rice is cooked in the traditional way in large pots (although now electric rice cookers are often used) some grain invariably sticks to the bottom of the pot and burns. After all the non-burned rice is served, hot water is poured into the pot and boiled. This is then served as a digestive rice tea at the end of the meal. There are many versions of rice tea, and one can be made without first cooking and burning a pot of rice.

MAKES 3¾ CUPS

2 tablespoons uncooked long-grain rice
3¾ cups boiling water

❖ Put the rice into a small heavy skillet and cook over a medium-low heat, stirring, until the rice becomes flecked with dark patches and has a rich nutty aroma.

❖ Tip the rice into a saucepan, and add the boiling water. Return to a boil, then simmer for 1½ minutes. Cover and remove from the heat. Leave for 5 minutes, then strain and serve the tea while still hot.

INDEX